DEAD MAN'S FAITH:

SPIRITUAL DEATH, FAITH, AND REGENERATION IN EPHESIANS 2:1–10

A Thesis

Presented to

The Faculty of the Department of

New Testament Literature and Exegesis

Chafer Theological Seminary

In Partial Fulfillment

of the Requirements for the Degree

Master of Theology

by

Timothy R. Nichols

May 2004

Copyright © 2016 by Timothy R. Nichols

All rights reserved
Printed in the United States of America

No part of this book may be reproduced in any form or by any electronic or mechanical means, including information storage and retrieval systems, except for brief quotations in printed reviews, without the prior permission of the author.

Headwaters Christian Resources

PREFACE

It has been over a decade since this thesis was finished, and in that interval, a number of people have asked me if it was available. Each time, I've sent a pdf copy to them, wishing I had it in print, but also wanting to do a rewrite.

Since I wrote this, I've been a pastor, teacher, author, bus driver, massage therapist -- you know, the usual range of ministry jobs. I've been privileged to see demons leave, the sick healed, the poor fed, the wounded made whole. I've heard God speak to me and to others, from the wealthy and well-off to homeless guys holding cardboard signs -- truth be told, sometimes a lot clearer to the latter. More significant still, I have come to know God's good heart for His children, and for me in particular -- a lesson that somehow eluded me for most of my life. I've come a long way from the green, self-serious feller that penned this thesis.

I put off publication for years because I believe a rewrite would make it more accessible and useful, and because the tone of *everything* I write now is different than it was then. I understand God differently, and hear Him better, than I ever did then. It makes a big difference.

But I haven't had time to do the rewrite. I probably won't anytime soon, and God seems to be using the work in its present form anyhow. So it's long past time to get the talent out there in the marketplace rather than leaving it buried in the backyard for another decade. When the Master returns, I don't want to be *that* servant.

This is a master's thesis, so it's not particularly designed for ease of use. But I've had some practice helping people use it over the years, and here's the best directions I can give you:
- If you're just interested in the passage, go to chapters 2 and 3.
- If you're after the theological take-away, the core argument is all on page 74, and then you can work outward from there.
- If you're more interested in the methodology, it might serve you to tackle the appendix on BAR outlining first, and then go back and see the method in action in the main text.

I hope it's helpful to you.

Tim Nichols
All Saints' Day, Year of our Lord 2016
Englewood, Colorado

Accepted by the Faculty of the Chafer Theological Seminary in
partial fulfillment of the requirements for the degree Master of Theology

Examining Committee

_____

_____

ACKNOWLEDGEMENTS

God gave us a great gift when He revealed Himself in the pages of Scripture, and He has brought me great blessing through His Word in the process of working on this project. I write with the aim of passing some of that blessing on to my readers. Whatever treasure may lie in these pages is from the Word of God. Accordingly, if a reader finds blessing here, the blessing is from God, and the glory is His. Without Him we can do nothing.

Writing a thesis requires significant preparation, not all of which occurs at seminary. It is fitting to recognize the willing servants through whom God prepared me. This thesis represents the confluence of two separate lineages of service and study, and God was pleased to work through multiple generations on both sides. My thanks are due first to the many teachers who prepared me for coming to CTS.

Rev. Edd Nichols is my father, my first and most important instructor in the Word. His teaching reflected many years of labor and sacrifice to learn the Word at Florida Bible College, at Capitol Bible Seminary, and in his own private study. My mother, Kayleen Nichols, ably assisted him (e.g., before I could even talk, she read me the Scriptures by the pool of Capitol Bible Seminary). Their labor and faithfulness in teaching and modeling the Word have paid me handsome dividends. In my education in the Word, my family enjoyed the aid of Faith Bible Church in Sterling, Virginia.

I owe a great debt to those at Florida Bible College who trained my parents in the Word before my birth: Dr. A. Ray Stanford, the late Dr. Mark G. Cambron, and particularly Dr. Richard A. Seymour, with whom I am belatedly impressed. His faithful application of 2 Timothy 2:2 was the reason I heard his teaching from my parents before hearing it from him as a student at FBC. I am grateful to him and my other teachers at FBC, notably Hal Haller, who first told me that Greek could be fun (I believe it—now), and Chad Woodburn, whose doctrine and practice of the (by grace, through faith) abundant life embody biblical teaching to a degree matched by few.

Having thus prepared me, the Lord brought me to CTS, a second line of the Lord's diligent servants. Since this is the first Th.M. thesis at CTS, it is appropriate to mention those whose ministry laid the foundations for the seminary:

Our namesake Dr. Lewis Sperry Chafer, the visionary who founded the Evangelical Theological College (now Dallas Theological Seminary), whose high regard for Scripture, contagious love for the grace of God, and dedication to the Word, the Lord, and the ministry shine through every page of his published works.

Dr. George E. Meisinger, along with the original founders, who had a vision for a seminary where students could focus on the languages and theology without spending all their study time earning the money to pay for it.

Dr. Dale M. Wheeler, who invented a peerless exegetical method and made it accessible to students during his time at DTS.

Dr. John H. Niemelä, language professor extraordinaire, who recognized the significance of Dr. Wheeler's exegetical method, invested enormously in learning it at DTS, and continues to fine-tune and teach it in ever-more-transmissible forms at CTS, where it is a key foundational element for the upper-division curriculum (language, theology, preaching, and hermeneutics). Without his teaching and mentoring, this thesis would never have existed, and his aid with the last stages of the diagram was invaluable.

Dr. Stephen R. Lewis, now President of Rocky Mountain Bible College and Seminary, whose infectious passion for going "back to the text" suffused his every class at CTS, and whose teaching on hermeneutical theory remains unparalleled.

Finally, above all save the Lord, I owe more thanks than I could repay to my beautiful bride Kimberly, who endured a much-elongated courtship because of seminary, who agreed to marry me with the completion of this thesis still hanging over our heads, and whose zany humor helped me to laugh despite being wearied from much study. "A merry heart does good like a medicine," and without that medicine I could not have finished this project. "Many daughters have done well, but you excel them all."

To Kimberly, who
has waited with faith
and patience these five
long years for me to
finish this thesis.
I love you
more
than
words
can say.
When we lift a glass
to celebrate, the toast is to you.

For the two ways of contemplation are not unlike the two ways of action commonly spoken of by the ancients; the one plain and smooth in the beginning, and in the end impassable; the other rough and troublesome in the entrance, but after a while fair and even. So it is in contemplation; if a man will begin with certainties, he shall end in doubts; but if he will be content to begin with doubts, he shall end in certainties.

Sir Francis Bacon, *The Advancement of Learning*

Ad fontes!

Renaissance slogan

TABLE OF CONTENTS

ACKNOWLEDGEMENTS iii
DEDICATION vi

Chapter

1. INTRODUCTION 1
   The Origins of this Study 1
   The Importance of this Study 2
   The Method of this Study 3
2. GRAMMATICAL FRAMEWORK OF EPHESIANS 2:1–10 5
   Introduction 5
   Framework Principles 5
   The Framework 8
     Full Text
     Finding the Framework in 2:1-10
       Verse 1
       Verse 2
       Verse 3
       Verse 4
       Verse 5
       Verse 6
       Verse 7
       Verse 8
       Verse 9
       Verse 10
     Selection Rationale
     The Coherence of the Emphasized Text
   Conclusion 16
3. EXEGESIS OF EPHESIANS 2:1–10 19
   Introduction 19
   Preceding Context 20
   Ephesians 2:1–10 21
     Text
     Translation
     Bottom-Level Outline Statements
     Upper-Level Outline Statements
   Following Context 39
4. HIGHLIGHTS FROM THE INTERPRETIVE TRADITION 41
   Introduction 41
   Meaning of *You* and *We* 41
     Position A
     Position C
     A Mediate Position (E)

        Position D
        Position F
        Crucial Data
      Meaning of *Dead* and *Made Alive* 52
        The Essential Nature of the Terms
          Moral/Experiential
          Spiritual/Forensic
          Paul's Emphasis
        Death, Life, and Faith
          Reformed Theology
          Arminian Theology
          Common Ground Between Reformed and Arminian Theologies
        Crucial Data
      Relation of *By Grace you are Saved* to its Contexts 61
        By Grace You Are Saved in 2:5
        By Grace You Are Saved in 2:8
      Relation of "Through Faith" to its Context 65
      Conclusion 67
        The Identity of *You* and *We*
        The Meaning of *Dead* and *Made Alive*
        The Relation of *By Grace You Are Saved* to its Contexts
        The Relation of *Through Faith* to its Contexts

5.   THE *ORDO SALUTIS* IN EPHESIANS 2:1–10 70
      Introduction 70
      The Argument 70
        Syllogism One
        Syllogism Two
        Syllogism Three
        Syllogism Four
        Syllogism Five
        Syllogism Six
      Conclusion 74

6.   THE ANTECEDENT OF ΤΟΥΤΟ 76
      Introduction 76
      An Analysis of Wallace 77
        First and Second Views: Χάριτί or Πίστεως as Antecedents
        Fourth View: Καὶ Τοῦτο as Adverbial with no Antecedent
        Third View: "Grace-by-Faith Salvation" as Antecedent
      Finding the Correct Conceptual Referent 87
      Conclusion 89

7.   CONCLUSION 90
      Summary 90
      Areas for Further Study 91

APPENDIX 1: BAR OUTLINING 94
      Introduction 94
      Provenance 94

Principles	95
Boundary	
Assertion	
Relation	
The Iterative Nature of BAR	
Practice	98
Topic *versus* Comment	
Signpost *versus* Structural Marker	
Types of Outline Statements	
Sentence Structure in Outline Statements	
Conclusion	102
APPENDIX 2: FULL OUTLINE OF EPHESIANS 2:1–10	103
BIBLIOGRAPHY	106
Original Sources	107
Commentaries	107
Books	111
Periodicals	114
Unpublished Materials	115

CHAPTER 1

INTRODUCTION

THE ORIGINS OF THIS STUDY

In the spring of 2000, the author, a second-year Greek student at the time, was asked to present the exegetical method taught in the New Testament department of Chafer Theological Seminary to the National Teaching Pastors' Conference in Kansas City, Missouri. He selected Ephesians 2:1–10 to demonstrate the method, little dreaming of what he would learn there. The author's preparation for that event focused on the passage and its full context, not the commentary literature. (It would be another year before the author would make a concerted study of even a few commentaries on this passage.) The author first developed the argument this study will adduce during that time of study and meditation on the Word, and presented it in a paper titled "The CTS Exegetical Outlining Method"[1] at that conference. A revised version appeared in *CTS Journal* under the title "Reverse-Engineered Outlining: A Method for Epistolary Exegesis."[2] While the current version represents considerable refinement and research beyond the initial presentation, the points of data and essential argument remain substantially unchanged.

The theological conclusion of this study rises from an unadorned exegesis of the text. A reader with no prior theological training, nor linguistic expertise, can discover it

---

[1] The author was then unaware that the methodology did *not* originate at CTS. John Niemelä learned it at DTS and further refined both the methodology itself and the means of transmission to students.

[2] Timothy R. Nichols, "Reverse-Engineered Outlining: A Method for Epistolary Exegesis," *CTS Journal* 7 (April–June 2001): 16–58.

in any quality English translation. While the commentaries have done much to raise issues for consideration, they have added nothing essential to the argument at issue or to the data on which stands. In fact, as this study will demonstrate, they tend to agree with the points of data, but fail to draw the necessary implication.

THE IMPORTANCE OF THIS STUDY

To judge from the breadth and diversity of the available literature, every passage of Scripture has functioned as a battleground on which countless conflicts have been fought, for equally countless reasons. The three sentences of Ephesians 2:1–10 are surely no exception; there has been no lack of study on this passage Chafer calls "the central passage of the Bible on divine grace."[3] However, a remarkable feature about the paragraph is how little serious conflict exists among Protestants over its import. To be sure, at some points opinions vary wildly from one commentator to the next, but at the pivot points of the passage, a careful reader finds much less variance.

Like the Scriptures from which they ostensibly come, the various theological categories of Christendom have occasioned countless battles. The *ordo salutis*,[4] particularly the temporal/logical relationship between regeneration and faith, has been one of the more well-worn battlegrounds. Unlike the passage under discussion here, no significant agreement seems to exist about the pivot points of this crucial doctrine.

---

[3] Lewis Sperry Chafer, "Dispensationalism," *Bibliotheca Sacra* 93 (October–December 1936); electronic reprint (Garland, TX: Galaxie, 2002), 427.

[4] *Ordo salutis* is a technical term literally meaning "order of salvation." Charles C. Ryrie, *Basic Theology* (Wheaton, IL: Victor, 1986), 536–37, defines it as "the attempt to arrange in logical (not temporal) order the activities involved in applying salvation to the individual."

This study juxtaposes those two elements (Ephesians 2:1–10 and the *ordo salutis*, particularly the relationship among death, faith, and regeneration) in order to demonstrate what the former indicates about the latter. Make no mistake: this text does indicate a particular order between regeneration and faith. The surprising truth is that although the inference regarding the *ordo salutis* is rarely if ever noticed here, the points of textual data on which the inference rests are widely acknowledged. Consequently, although a number of useful treatments of the passage exist, the portrayal of Paul's basic meaning remains incomplete. This is partly because many interpreters attach more to the definition of a particular word in the passage than the context can support. But the text itself corrects this mistake. So the oversight results less from a widespread interpretive error than from ignoring a basic implication of the widely accepted interpretation. This study seeks to remedy that situation.

THE METHOD OF THIS STUDY

This study begins, as all theological study properly should, with exegesis of the text at hand. Chapter 2 will focus on the grammatical structure of the passage, and Chapter 3 will focus on exegesis. The theological argument of the study depends only upon seven points of data within the passage, so every exegetical point is not central to this thesis. The degree of space invested in validation will vary accordingly. However, these seven points should be understood within their context, and a full exegesis of the passage will give the reader a frame of reference within which to view the essential points. Chapter 4 will survey the literature on those seven points of data, demonstrating that surprisingly little important variance exists within the commentary tradition. Chapter 5 will develop the theological argument in six syllogisms based on the textual data. Theologians and commentators frequently adduce Ephesians 2:8 as evidence that faith is a gift from God. Since that proposition bears indirectly on the argument of this thesis, Chapter 6 will discuss the antecedent of τοῦτο in that verse. Finally—and fittingly for a thesis at *Chafer* Theological Seminary—a seventh chapter will conclude the thesis, summarizing the argument and offering suggestions for further research.

CHAPTER 2

GRAMMATICAL FRAMEWORK OF EPHESIANS 2:1–10

INTRODUCTION

Paul's letter to the Ephesians is Scripture. Every word of it is breathed by God, written down by a holy man borne along by the Holy Spirit. *Every word of it matters.* Precisely because that is the case, an interpreter must correctly understand its structure. In any complex sentence, certain propositions provide the skeleton, as it were, that shapes and defines the rest of the sentence. One must ultimately interpret the sentence in its entirety, but that process necessarily begins with the grammatical core (main verb, subject, and any object[1]). Only then can an interpreter proceed outward from the core to the modifying material that surrounds it.

FRAMEWORK PRINCIPLES

While the second and third sentences of Ephesians 2:1–10 are fairly simple, the first is quite complex. Interpretation of the sentence must begin with an understanding of the grammar, so the complexities of 2:1–7 justify spending time to clarify how the grammatical framework of the passage works, i.e., where the core propositions lie and how the modifying material relates grammatically to them. All modifying material is not created equal: some things can drop out and the sentence will still make perfect sense. Other modifiers lie closer to the heart of the sentence's meaning: dropping them out of the sentence may not materially affect the grammar of the sentence (i.e., it will still be a

---

[1] Or predicate substantive/predicate adjective, in the case of a stative verb.

grammatically well-formed sentence), but the sentence will make less sense.[2] Some components, however, cannot be dropped out of the sentence without destroying it. The grammatical core of a sentence is the independent clause at its heart, which appears on the baseline of a grammatical diagram. For example, for 2:1–7, the following diagram shows the baseline:

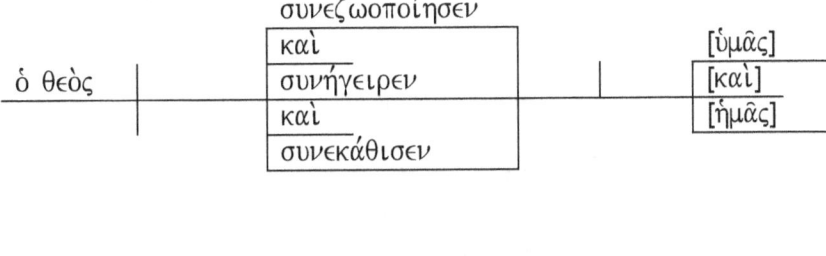

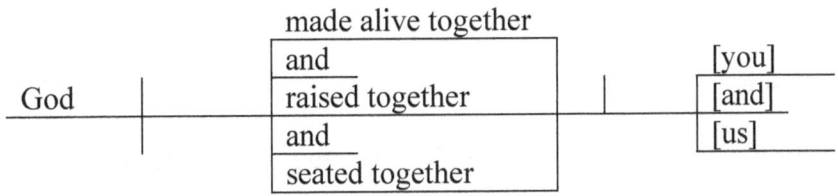

From the core proposition (shown on the baseline of the diagram), one can proceed outward, arranging the modifying material of the sentence in order of grammatical proximity, as illustrated by the chart on page 7. Everything that appears on the full grammatical diagrams belongs to one of the categories on that chart.

---

[2] Being grammatically well-formed differs from being coherent. By way of illustration, the sentence "Moons write brave cabinets" meets all the requirements for an independent clause. It has a verb (*write*), a subject (*moons*), and is not a dependent clause. (For example, "If moons write brave cabinets," could not be a complete sentence.) In addition, it has a direct object (*cabinets*), modified by an adjective (*brave*). It is a grammatically well-formed sentence, even though it means absolutely nothing.

Grammatical Proximity

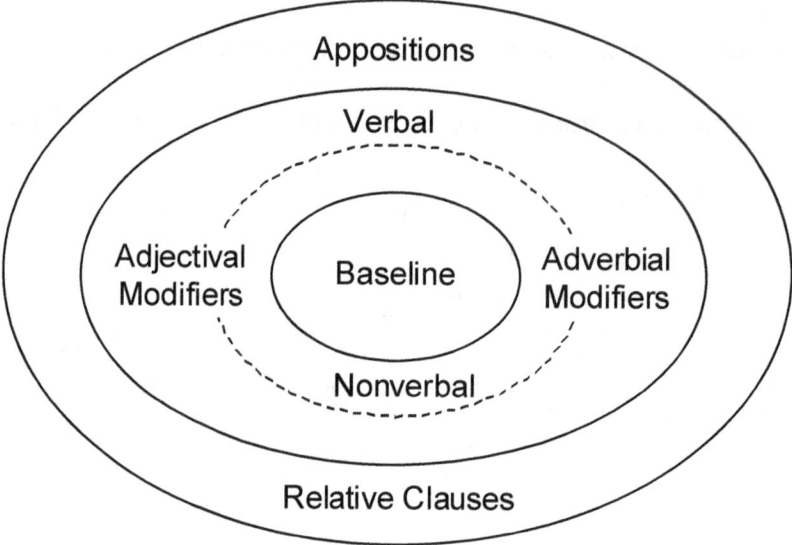

Most closely related to the core proposition of the sentence are the nonverbal modifiers that attach to the baseline. For example, dropping τῷ Χριστῷ in 2:5 from the sentence would not compromise its grammatical integrity as an independent clause, but it would lose clarity. The verbs all have a συν- prefix,[3] which raises the question, "Together with whom?" Even though its grammatical integrity remains intact, the sentence lacks something if it fails to answer that question.

Next in order of proximity are the verbal modifiers.[4] These are often full clauses in their own right, with objects, modifiers, and (frequently implicit) subjects of their own.

---

[3] Συν is a Greek preposition meaning *with* or *together with*. Greek often creates a compound verb by prefixing a preposition to a verb form.

[4] Verbal modifiers include participial and infinitival clauses as well as finite verbs introduced by subordinating conjunctions.

The latter create a "nesting" effect: a complex sentence will have modifiers of its modifiers of its modifiers, *ad infinitum*.

Furthest away in terms of grammatical proximity are the relative clauses that modify some portion of the sentence. By definition, relative clauses are grammatically independent, but logically dependent through the pronoun. These appear on the diagram in dotted lines.

Accordingly, the following examination of the grammar of Ephesians 2:1–10 will show how the framework fits together. It will begin with the full text of the passage, then proceed verse by verse, examining each part to show its grammatical relation to the core proposition of its sentence. It will conclude with an abbreviated text of the passage based on the core propositions and certain modifying material.

THE FRAMEWORK

Full Text

The table below contains the full text of Ephesians 2:1–10,[5] with a parallel translation by the author.

Full Text and Translation	
₁ Καὶ ὑμᾶς ὄντας νεκροὺς τοῖς παραπτώμασιν καὶ ταῖς ἁμαρτίαις,	₁ And you, being dead in trespasses and sins,
₂ ἐν αἷς ποτε περιεπατήσατε κατὰ τὸν αἰῶνα τοῦ κόσμου τούτου, κατὰ τὸν ἄρχοντα τῆς ἐξουσίας τοῦ ἀέρος, τοῦ πνεύματος τοῦ νῦν ἐνεργοῦντος ἐν τοῖς υἱοῖς τῆς ἀπειθείας·	₂ among which you once walked according to the age of this world, according to the prince of the power of the air, the spirit now working in the sons of disobedience

---

[5] Original text is from Zane C. Hodges and Arthur L. Farstad, eds., *The Greek New Testament According to the Majority Text*, 2nd ed. (Nashville, TN: Nelson, 1985), 584.

Full Text and Translation	
3 ἐν οἷς καὶ ἡμεῖς πάντες ἀνεστράφημέν ποτε ἐν ταῖς ἐπιθυμίαις τῆς σαρκὸς ἡμῶν, ποιοῦντες τὰ θελήματα τῆς σαρκὸς καὶ τῶν διανοιῶν, καὶ ἦμεν τέκνα φύσει ὀργῆς ὡς καὶ οἱ λοιποί·	3 among whom we all also formerly conducted ourselves in the lusts of our flesh, doing the will of the flesh and of the mind, and were by nature children of wrath, as *were* also the rest
4 ὁ δὲ θεός, πλούσιος ὢν ἐν ἐλέει, διὰ τὴν πολλὴν ἀγάπην αὐτοῦ ἣν ἠγάπησεν ἡμᾶς,	4 but God, being rich in mercy because of His great love with which He loved us;
5 καὶ ὄντας ἡμᾶς νεκροὺς τοῖς παραπτώμασιν, συνεζωοποίησεν τῷ Χριστῷ—χάριτί ἐστε σεσῳσμένοι—	5 we also being dead in sins, made *you and us* alive together with Christ—by grace you are saved—
6 καὶ συνήγειρεν καὶ συνεκάθισεν ἐν τοῖς ἐπουρανίοις ἐν Χριστῷ Ἰησοῦ,	6 and raised *you and us* together and seated *you and us* together in the heavenlies in Christ
7 ἵνα ἐνδείξηται ἐν τοῖς αἰῶσιν τοῖς ἐπερχομένοις τὸν ὑπερβάλλοντα πλοῦτον τῆς χάριτος αὐτοῦ ἐν χρηστότητι ἐφ ἡμᾶς ἐν Χριστῷ Ἰησοῦ.	7 in order that He might demonstrate in the coming ages the overwhelming riches of His grace in kindness toward us in Christ Jesus.
8 Τῇ γὰρ χάριτί ἐστε σεσῳσμένοι διὰ τῆς πίστεως· καὶ τοῦτο οὐκ ἐξ ὑμῶν, θεοῦ τὸ δῶρον·	8 For by grace you are saved through faith, and this *is* not of yourselves, *but is* a gift of God,
9 οὐκ ἐξ ἔργων, ἵνα μή τις καυχήσηται.	9 not of works, lest anyone should boast.
10 Αὐτοῦ γάρ ἐσμεν ποίημα, κτισθέντες ἐν Χριστῷ Ἰησοῦ ἐπὶ ἔργοις ἀγαθοῖς οἷς προητοίμασεν ὁ θεὸς ἵνα ἐν αὐτοῖς περιπατήσωμεν.	10 For we are His artifact, created in Christ Jesus unto good works, which God previously prepared in order that we might walk in them.

Finding the Framework in 2:1–10

This segment of the chapter will function as a brief grammatical commentary on Ephesians 2:1–10. Discussion of line weights refers to the diagrams on pages 17–18. Readers will profit from following along on the diagrams.

Verse 1. The καὶ that begins the verse relates this whole paragraph to the preceding paragraph (1:15–23). It is crucial to the placement of 2:1–10 in the book as a whole, but does not relate elements within the paragraph.[6] The concessive participle ὄντας modifies the three main verbs in 2:5–6. Ὑμᾶς is its subject, νεκροὺς its predicate accusative adjective,[7] and the remainder of the verse an adverbial prepositional phrase modifying ὄντας. The concessive clause appears in bold lines on the diagram.[8]

Verse 2. Verse 2 is a relative clause. The relative pronoun αἷς, which refers to ταῖς ἁμαρτίαις in verse 1, is the object of ἐν. The prepositional phrase modifies the main verb of the clause, περιεπατήσατε. The two phrases beginning with κατὰ also modify the verb. Τοῦ πνεύματος stands in apposition to the object of the second κατὰ phrase. The adjectival participle ἐνεργοῦντος modifies πνεύματος, and the ἐν phrase modifies the participle. Thus the whole of verse 2 is bound up in a relative clause, and appears on dotted lines in the diagram.

Verse 3. Verse 3 is also a long relative clause. The relative pronoun οἷς, referring to τοῖς υἱοῖς τῆς ἀπειθείας in verse 2, is the object of the preposition ἐν. The prepositional phrase modifies the first of two main verbs, ἀνεστράφημέν. The first main

---

[6] I.e., it is a signpost. See Appendix 1, esp. pages 99–100, for discussion

[7] Terminology is a problem here. Exegetes tend to use *predicate nominative* and *predicate adjective* as mutually exclusive categories, which they are not, since predicate adjectives can be nominative. (Properly opposite terms would be *predicate substantive* and *predicate adjective*.) The false dichotomy also treats *predicate genitive*, *predicate dative*, and *predicate accusative* as predicate substantives. The imprecise distinction creates problems in a case like this one, because νεκροὺς is a predicate accusative as well as a predicate adjective.

[8] See discussion pages 13–14.

verb is also modified by a second ἐν phrase and a participial modifier (ποιοῦντες . . . διανοιῶν). Καὶ connects the first main verb with the second, ἤμεν, which precedes its predicate nominative τέκνα and its adverbial modifiers φύσει and the ὡς clause. As a relative clause, verse 3 also appears on dotted lines in the diagram.

Verse 4. The δέ contrasts the participial modifier that follows to the concessive material in 2:1–3. Θεός is the subject of the sentence, and appears on bold lines in the diagram because it is part of the core proposition. The ὤν clause modifies the main verbs and appears on medium-weight lines because it is a verbal modifier. The final three words of the verse are a relative clause explaining ἀγάπην. Like the other relative clauses, this one appears on dotted lines.

Verse 5. Καὶ ὄντας . . . παραπτώμασιν is a second concessive participial clause, parallel to verse 1. Like verse 1, it appears on bold lines for reasons discussed later. Συνεζωοποίησεν is the first of the three main verbs, and appears on bold lines because it is part of the core proposition. Τῷ Χριστῷ is the modifier required to complete the idea of the συν- prefix. Like all non-verbal modifiers of a core proposition, it appears on bold lines. The juxtaposition of the concessive modifiers and this verb implies a pair of direct objects, ὑμᾶς and ἡμᾶς, for the three main verbs (συνεζωοποίησεν . . . καὶ συνήγειρεν καὶ συνεκάθισεν). Χάριτί ἐστε σεσῳσμένοι is parenthetical, i.e., grammatically unconnected to the rest of the sentence, as the diagram shows.[9] Its relation to its context is a major

---

[9] Thanks are in order to John H. Niemelä, "*If Anyone's Work Is Burned*: Scrutinizing Proof-Texts," *CTS Journal* 8 (January–March 2002): 22–42, for suggesting the insertion of the parenthetic clause between the first two main verbs on the diagram (as it appears also in the text).

issue in this thesis, and will receive extensive discussion elsewhere.[10] Because it is a core proposition in its own right, it appears on bold lines.

Verse 6. Verse 6 contains the sentence's remaining main verbs, linked by καὶ. They share the subject θεὸς and implicit direct objects ὑμᾶς and ἡμᾶς with συνεζωοποίησεν. Following them are two adverbial prepositional phrases. As part of the core proposition or its nonverbal modifiers, all parts of verse 6 appear on bold lines.[11]

Verse 7. Verse 7 is a single ἵνα clause that modifies the main verbs. The clause contains a finite verb (ἐνδείξηται), its object (πλοῦτον) and a mass of modifying material, both adverbial and adjectival. Since it is a verbal modifier, this clause appears on medium-weight lines in the diagram. This clause concludes the first sentence.

Verse 8. Γὰρ is a signpost marking the relation of the new sentence to the preceding one. This sentence opens by repeating the parenthesis from verse 5.[12] Διὰ τῆς πίστεως is an adverbial prepositional phrase modifying the main verb. Καὶ links verse 8a to a second independent clause. The subject is τοῦτο, and it has three implicit main verbs, all ἐστιν. The first is modified by οὐκ ἐξ ὑμῶν, and the second has τὸ δῶρον as its predicate nominative. The position of the positive statement between the negative (οὐκ) statements requires repeating the implicit ἐστιν. As part of the core proposition or nonverbal modifier, all of verse 8 appears on bold lines.

---

[10] See pages 61–63.

[11] Niemelä, "*Anyone's Work*," 28, also discusses the core proposition of this sentence.

[12] Regarding Paul's addition of the article τῇ, see discussion page 64.

Verse 9. Οὐκ ἐξ ἔργων modifies the third implicit ἐστιν. This clause is part of the core proposition, so it appears on bold lines. The remainder of verse 9 is a ἵνα clause modifying all three implicit verbs. As a verbal modifier, it appears on medium-weight lines.

Verse 10. Verse 10 is the third and final sentence in the paragraph. Γάρ is a signpost linking it with the preceding sentence. The core proposition is a stative verb (with implicit subject) and predicate nominative (ἐσμεν ποίημα), and appears on bold lines. All else is modifying material. Αὐτοῦ modifies ποίημα. The participle κτισθέντες modifies the main verb. The ἐν and ἐπὶ phrases modify the participle. As a verbal modifier, the entire participial clause appears on medium-weight lines. Οἷς begins a relative clause, adverbially modified in turn by the ἵνα clause that closes the sentence, so it appears on dotted lines.

Selection Rationale

This study will emphasize certain aspects of the text over others, according to two criteria: grammatical proximity to the core propositions of the paragraph and logical necessity for this study. It will, of course, emphasize the core propositions in all three sentences and all nonverbal modifiers to those propositions. It will not emphasize the material contained in the relative clauses, because it stands at the grammatical periphery and does not bear directly on the argument of this study. Between those two extremes lie the verbal modifiers. Here selection varies according to logical necessity for this study. The concessive participles will receive emphasis because of their juxtaposition with the first main verb (*being dead* and *made alive together*) and their critical importance to the argument of this study regarding the meaning of *dead* and *made alive*. However, the causal participle in 2:4, the ἵνα clauses in 2:7 and 2:9, and the participial modifier in 2:10 will not receive emphasis because they do not bear directly on the argument of this study. The chart below shows the emphasized portions of the text in underlined, boldface type.

Finding the Framework: Text and Translation	
₁ <u>Καὶ ὑμᾶς ὄντας νεκροὺς τοῖς παραπτώμασιν καὶ ταῖς ἁμαρτίαις,</u>	₁ **<u>And you, being dead in trespasses and sins,</u>**
₂ ἐν αἷς ποτε περιεπατήσατε κατὰ τὸν αἰῶνα τοῦ κόσμου τούτου, κατὰ τὸν ἄρχοντα τῆς ἐξουσίας τοῦ ἀέρος, τοῦ πνεύματος τοῦ νῦν ἐνεργοῦντος ἐν τοῖς υἱοῖς τῆς ἀπειθείας·	₂ among which you once walked according to the age of this world, according to the prince of the power of the air, the spirit now working in the sons of disobedience
₃ ἐν οἷς καὶ ἡμεῖς πάντες ἀνεστράφημέν ποτε ἐν ταῖς ἐπιθυμίαις τῆς σαρκὸς ἡμῶν, ποιοῦντες τὰ θελήματα τῆς σαρκὸς καὶ τῶν διανοιῶν, καὶ ἤμεν τέκνα φύσει ὀργῆς ὡς καὶ οἱ λοιποί·	₃ among whom we all also formerly conducted ourselves in the lusts of our flesh, doing the will of the flesh and of the mind, and were by nature children of wrath, as were also the rest
₄ ὁ δὲ <u>θεὸς,</u>πλούσιος ὢν ἐν ἐλέει,διὰ τὴν πολλὴν ἀγάπην αὐτοῦ ἣν ἠγάπησεν ἡμᾶς,	₄ but **<u>God,</u>** being rich in mercy because of His great love with which He loved us;
₅ <u>καὶ ὄντας ἡμᾶς νεκροὺς τοῖς παραπτώμασιν, συνεζωοποίησεν τῷ Χριστῷ — χάριτί ἐστε σεσωσμένοι —</u>	₅ **<u>we also being dead in sins, made *you and us* alive together with Christ — by grace you are saved —</u>**
₆ <u>καὶ συνήγειρεν καὶ συνεκάθισεν ἐν τοῖς ἐπουρανίοις ἐν Χριστῷ Ἰησοῦ,</u>	₆ **<u>and raised *you and us* together and seated *you and us* together in the heavenlies in Christ</u>**
₇ ἵνα ἐνδείξηται ἐν τοῖς αἰῶσιν τοῖς ἐπερχομένοις τὸν ὑπερβάλλοντα πλοῦτον τῆς χάριτος αὐτοῦ ἐν χρηστότητι ἐφ ἡμᾶς ἐν Χριστῷ Ἰησοῦ.	₇ in order that He might demonstrate in the coming ages the overwhelming riches of His grace in kindness toward us in Christ Jesus.
₈ <u>Τῇ γὰρ χάριτί ἐστε σεσωσμένοι διὰ τῆς πίστεως· καὶ τοῦτο οὐκ ἐξ ὑμῶν, θεοῦ τὸ δῶρον·</u>	₈ **<u>For by grace you are saved through faith, and this *is* not of yourselves, *but is* a gift of God,</u>**
₉ <u>οὐκ ἐξ ἔργων,</u> ἵνα μή τις καυχήσηται.	₉ **<u>not of works,</u>** lest anyone should boast.
₁₀ <u>Αὐτοῦ γάρ ἐσμεν ποίημα,</u> κτισθέντες ἐν Χριστῷ Ἰησοῦ ἐπὶ ἔργοις ἀγαθοῖς οἷς προητοίμασεν ὁ θεὸς ἵνα ἐν αὐτοῖς περιπατήσωμεν.	₁₀ **<u>For we are His artifact,</u>** created in Christ Jesus unto good works, which God previously prepared in order that we might walk in them.

The Coherence of the Emphasized Text

The emphasized text forms a grammatically coherent whole. The word order makes it difficult to demonstrate this fact in parallel translation, but a glance at the grammatical diagrams[13] or the smoother translation below the chart will confirm it. The chart below contains only the text being emphasized in this study.

Emphasized Text and Translation	
1 Καὶ ὑμᾶς ὄντας νεκροὺς τοῖς παραπτώμασιν καὶ ταῖς ἁμαρτίαις . . .	1 And you, being dead in trespasses and sins . . .
4 ὁ . . . θεὸς, . . .	4 God, . . .
5 καὶ ὄντας ἡμᾶς νεκροὺς τοῖς παραπτώμασιν, συνεζωοποίησεν τῷ Χριστῷ — χάριτί ἐστε σεσῳσμένοι —	5 we also being dead in sins, made *you and us* alive together with Christ — by grace you are saved —
6 καὶ συνήγειρεν καὶ συνεκάθισεν ἐν τοῖς ἐπουρανίοις ἐν Χριστῷ Ἰησοῦ. . . .	6 and raised *you and us* together and seated *you and us* together in the heavenlies in Christ. . . .
8 Τῇ γὰρ χάριτί ἐστε σεσῳσμένοι διὰ τῆς πίστεως· καὶ τοῦτο οὐκ ἐξ ὑμῶν, θεοῦ τὸ δῶρον·	8 For by grace you are saved through faith, and this *is* not of yourselves, *but is a* gift of God,
9 οὐκ ἐξ ἔργων. . . .	9 not of works. . . .
10 Αὐτοῦ γάρ ἐσμεν ποίημα. . . .	10 For we are His artifact. . . .

A smoother translation of the emphasized text might read as follows:

Although you were dead in trespasses and sins, and we also were dead in sins, God made you and us alive together with Christ — by grace you are saved — and raised you and us together, and seated you and us together in the heavenlies in Christ. For by grace you are saved through faith, and this is not from yourselves, but is a gift of God, not of works. For we are His artifact.

---

[13] See pages 17–18.

The above translation demonstrates that the portion of the text this study will emphasize is a coherent whole. It contains, in germ, the argument of the whole paragraph.[14] As the full exegesis in the next chapter will show, the de-emphasized material will add certain dimensions to, but not alter, the argument of the passage as portrayed in the above translation.

CONCLUSION

A proper understanding of the passage begins with isolating the core propositions and working outward from there. While one must interpret the passage as a whole, the grammatical framework gives shape to it just as the skeleton gives shape to the body. Therefore a correct understanding of that framework has priority in exegesis. This study will cover the entire text of 2:1–10, but it will emphasize the core propositions and the concessive clauses that are juxtaposed to the first main verb. This emphasis accords with the grammar and contains the argument of the whole passage in germ. In addition, the points of data that fuel the theological argument of this study all appear in the emphasized portion of the text.

---

[14] For further discussion of the argument's development, see pages 19–40.

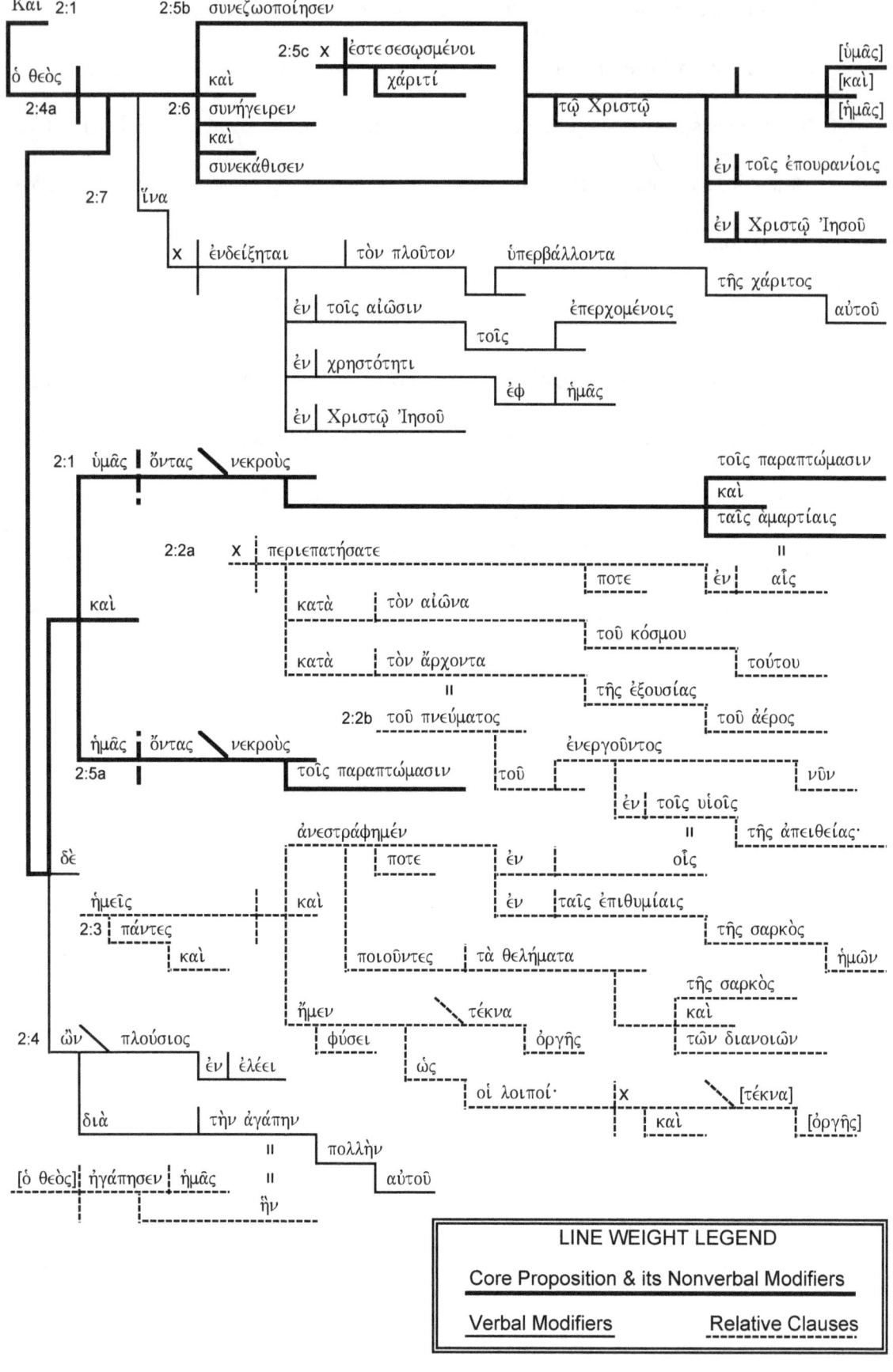

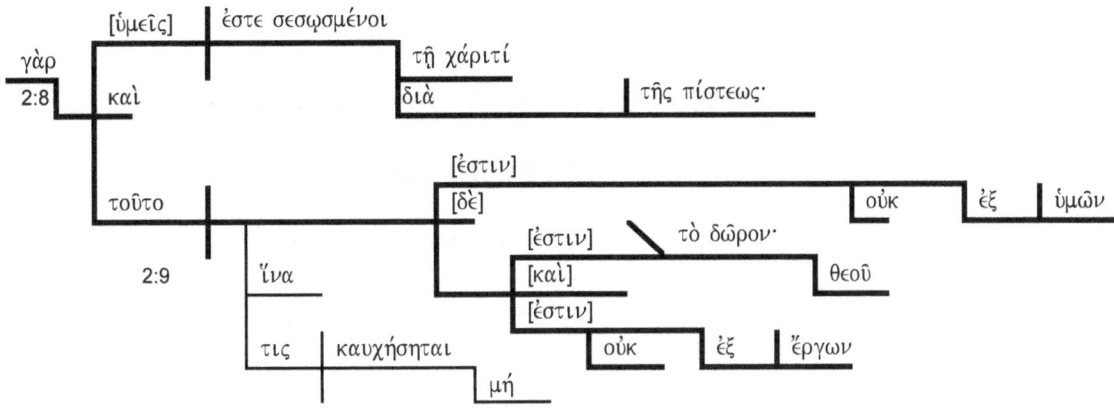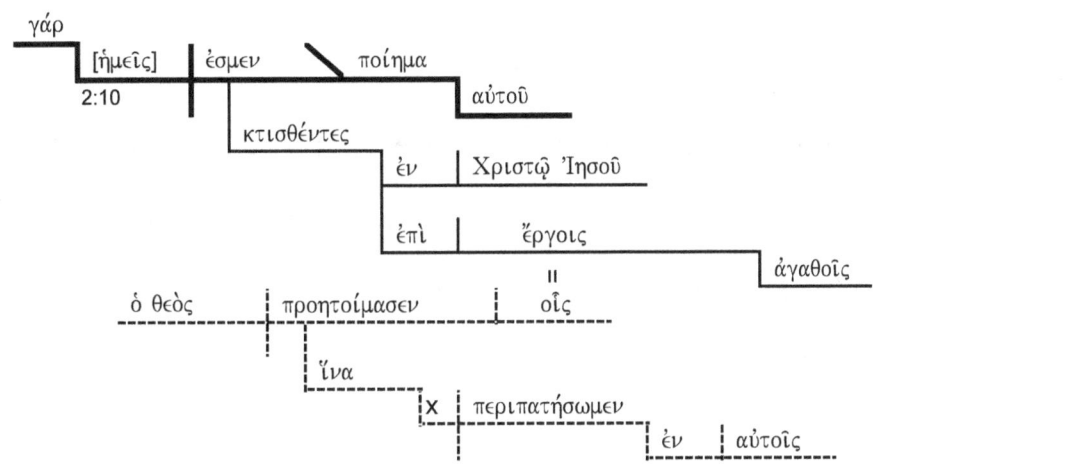

CHAPTER 3

EXEGESIS OF EPHESIANS 2:1–10

INTRODUCTION

In order to place the passage in its context, this chapter will begin with a brief survey of the preceding context. A full exegesis of Ephesians 2:1–10 will follow that survey. The format of the exegesis will follow the BAR exegetical outlining method[1] taught at CTS, i.e., it will focus on propositions, and the outline will proceed from the bottom level (i.e., details) upward to the top (i.e., overall point). Outline levels will be indicated by the Grace/Talbot method.[2] After the exegesis of 2:1–10, a concluding section will survey the remainder of the doctrinal section (2:11–3:21) and the pivot point of the book (4:1–6), which relates the doctrine in 1:3–3:21 to the practical instructions to follow (4:7–6:20).

---

[1] The acronym BAR stands for Boundary, Assertion, and Relation, the three key principles of this method of outlining. Timothy R. Nichols, "Reverse-Engineered Outlining: A Method for Epistolary Exegesis," *CTS Journal* 7 (April–June 2001): 16–58, explains this system, albeit with a less-developed nomenclature. Appendix 1 explains the essential principles in current nomenclature.

[2] This outlining convention originated at Grace Theological Seminary and then spread to Talbot Theological Seminary. Josh McDowell further popularized it in his works *Evidence that Demands a Verdict* (N.p.: Campus Crusade, 1972) and *More Evidence that Demands a Verdict* (N.p.: Campus Crusade, 1975). In the Grace/Talbot method, letters in the alphabet represent the level of the outline point, while numbers differentiate points at the same level. This system simplifies reference to a whole level of points, e.g., one speaks of "E-level points" rather than "Arabic-numeral-in-parentheses-level points." A side-by-side comparison of conventional and Grace/Talbot methods appears below.

```
I.                                      1A.
    A.                                      1B.
        1.                                      1C.
            a)                                      1D.
                (1)                                     1E.
                (2)                                     2E.
            b)                                      2D.
        2.                                      2C.
    B.                                      2B.
II.                                     2A.
```

This chapter will provide a positive presentation of the entire context in which the later theological argument takes place. The theological conclusion of this study rests directly on seven points in the passage. Chapter 4 will focus on validation of those seven points; this chapter will establish the context within which those validations can occur.

PRECEDING CONTEXT[3]

After his initial greeting, Paul opens the body of the epistle by enjoining[4] his Gentile audience to praise the Father[5] (1) for His role in planning and preparing the salvation of the Jews,[6] to the praise of the glory of His grace, (2) for the Son's role in carrying out the salvation of the Jews, which will culminate in His eschatological dominion over all things and their attendant inheritance in Him, to the praise of the Father's[7] glory—in which salvation the Gentile[8] believers also partake—and (3) for the Spirit's role in securing the destiny of Gentile and Jewish believers, to the praise of the

---

[3] Long sentences in this section stem from the BAR format and reflect Paul's long sentences in the Greek text.

[4] The form of "be" in 1:3a is not stated, so the mood of the verb is open to question. Is it indicative (*God is blessed*) or imperative (*Let God be blessed*)? If the former, Paul informs his audience of the blessedness of God, implying that they ought to admire and adore Him. If the latter, then the verse directly commands blessing God.

[5] Note that the beginning and ending paragraphs of the doctrinal section, 1:3–14 and 3:20–21, form a benedictory *inclusio*.

[6] See page 49 for discussion of *you* and *we* as references to Gentiles and Jews, respectively.

[7] The focus of the main clause (*Blessed be God the Father*) suggests that the pronoun *His* in 1:12, 14 refers to the Father as well. The fact that the benediction in 3:20–21 also has a paterological focus is significant, because 1:3–14 and 3:20–21 form an *inclusio*.

[8] 1:12–14 is the first of several key passages where Paul contrasts *you* and *we* (cf. 2:1–3, 11–18; 3:1–13). Some find it odd that Paul would so emphasize Jewish salvation when addressing a Gentile audience. But this is a historically accurate presentation of the order in which those groups came to faith (Acts 11:15–18). It also accords with Jesus' teaching (John 4:22) and Paul's theology and normal order of presentation: to the Jew first, and also to the Greek (Acts 13:46; Rom. 1:16; 2:9–10; 10:16–25).

Father's glory.[9] He then offers a prayer that God, having already enlightened his readers, will reveal to them the expectation to which He called them, the rich inheritance He lays up for them, and the greatness of His power that works in them—the same power that raised Christ from the dead and seated Him in the heavenlies, in dominion over all powers for all time.[10] In addition, the Father has placed all things under Christ's feet, and in particular made Him absolute head over the church, which is Christ's body and fullness.[11]

EPHESIANS 2:1–10

***Text*[12]**

₁ Καὶ ὑμᾶς ὄντας νεκροὺς τοῖς παραπτώμασιν καὶ ταῖς ἁμαρτίαις,[13] ₂ ἐν αἷς ποτε περιεπατήσατε κατὰ τὸν αἰῶνα τοῦ κόσμου τούτου, κατὰ τὸν ἄρχοντα τῆς ἐξουσίας τοῦ ἀέρος, τοῦ πνεύματος τοῦ νῦν ἐνεργοῦντος ἐν τοῖς υἱοῖς τῆς ἀπειθείας· ₃ ἐν οἷς καὶ ἡμεῖς πάντες ἀνεστράφημέν ποτε ἐν ταῖς ἐπιθυμίαις τῆς σαρκὸς ἡμῶν, ποιοῦντες τὰ θελήματα τῆς σαρκὸς καὶ τῶν διανοιῶν, καὶ ἦμεν[14] τέκνα φύσει ὀργῆς ὡς καὶ οἱ λοιποί· ₄ ὁ δὲ θεός, πλούσιος ὢν ἐν ἐλέει, διὰ τὴν πολλὴν ἀγάπην αὐτοῦ ἣν

---

[9] 1:3–14.

[10] 1:15–21.

[11] 1:22–23.

[12] The text is from Zane C. Hodges and Arthur L. Farstad, eds., *The Greek New Testament According to the Majority Text*, 2nd ed. (Nashville, TN: Nelson, 1985), 584. Use of bold subscript for verse numbers allows for standard footnoting of the text. For citation of textual variants, when the footnotes refer to "critical-text editions," evidence derives from the texts of *The Greek New Testament*, 4th ed., edited by Barbara Aland, Kurt Aland, Johannes Karavidopoulos, Carlo M. Martini, and Bruce Metzger (Stuttgart: Bibelstiftung, 1993); *Novum Testamentum Graece: Post Eberhard Nestle et Erwin Nestle*, 27th ed., edited by Barbara Aland, Kurt Aland, Johannes Karavidopoulos, Carlo M. Martini, and Bruce Metzger (Stuttgart: Bibelstiftung, 1993); Constantin von Tischendorf, ed., *Novum Testamentum Graece*, vol. 2 (Leipzig: Gieseke & Devrient, 1872; reprint, Graz: Akademische, 1965); and Brooke Foss Westcott and Fenton John Anthony Hort, eds., *The New Testament in the Original Greek* (New York: Harper, 1882; reprint, New York: Macmillan, 1949).

[13] Critical-text editions add ὑμῶν.

[14] Critical-text editions substitute ἤμεθα for ἦμεν.

ἠγάπησεν ἡμᾶς, ₅ καὶ ὄντας ἡμᾶς νεκροὺς τοῖς παραπτώμασιν, συνεζωοποίησεν¹⁵ τῷ Χριστῷ — χάριτί ἐστε σεσῳσμένοι — ₆ καὶ συνήγειρεν καὶ συνεκάθισεν ἐν τοῖς ἐπουρανίοις ἐν Χριστῷ Ἰησοῦ, ₇ ἵνα ἐνδείξηται ἐν τοῖς αἰῶσιν τοῖς ἐπερχομένοις τὸν ὑπερβάλλοντα πλοῦτον¹⁶ τῆς χάριτος αὐτοῦ ἐν χρηστότητι ἐφ ἡμᾶς ἐν Χριστῷ Ἰησοῦ. ₈ Τῇ γὰρ χάριτί ἐστε σεσῳσμένοι διὰ τῆς¹⁷ πίστεως· καὶ τοῦτο οὐκ ἐξ ὑμῶν, θεοῦ τὸ δῶρον· ₉ οὐκ ἐξ ἔργων, ἵνα μή τις καυχήσηται. ₁₀ Αὐτοῦ γάρ ἐσμεν ποίημα, κτισθέντες ἐν Χριστῷ Ἰησοῦ ἐπὶ ἔργοις ἀγαθοῖς οἷς προητοίμασεν ὁ θεὸς ἵνα ἐν αὐτοῖς περιπατήσωμεν.

Translation[18]

₁ And you, being dead in trespasses and sins, ₂ among which you once walked according to the age of this world, according to the prince of the power of the air, the spirit now working in the sons of disobedience ₃ among whom we all also formerly conducted ourselves in the lusts of our flesh, doing the will of the flesh and of the mind, and were by nature children of wrath, as *were* also the rest ₄ but God, being rich in mercy because of His great love with which He loved us; ₅ we also being dead in sins, made *you and us* alive together with Christ — by grace you are saved — ₆ and raised *you and us* together and seated *you and us* together in the heavenlies in Christ ₇ in order that He might demonstrate in the coming ages the overwhelming riches of His grace in kindness toward us in Christ Jesus. ₈ For by grace you are saved through faith, and this *is* not of yourselves, *but* is a gift of God, ₉ not of works, lest anyone should boast. ₁₀ For we are his artifact,[19] created in Christ Jesus unto good works, which God previously prepared in order that we might walk in them.

Bottom-Level Outline Statements

The format of an outline statement is as follows: first, in brackets, the structural marker from the Greek text that indicates the textual unit's relation to its context.

---

[15] The marginal reading of Wescott and Hort, *New Testament*, 431, inserts ἐν.

[16] Critical-text editions substitute τὸ ὑπερβάλλον πλοῦτος for τὸν ὑπερβάλλοντα πλοῦτον.

[17] Critical-text editions omit the article.

[18] The translation is the author's. The sentence breaks in the translation reflect the sentence breaks in the Greek text—an uncommon feature in English translations of this passage.

[19] The more common translation *workmanship* detracts from the singular nature of ποίημα. The sense is that *we* collectively, Jewish and Gentile believers alike, are a single work fashioned by God.

Second, an indicative-mood assertion paraphrases the unit of text. If the unit is dependent[20] on another clause, the outline statement must also state the unit's relationship to its topic.[21] Any elements in the assertion that derive from context, but not appear in the unit of text itself, must appear in brackets. Finally, a verse reference in parentheses concludes the statement. The bottom-level outline statements[22] appear in boldface type below. The paragraph(s) of plain text following the outline statement contain commentary on the unit of text covered by that statement. An asterisk precedes the outline statements dealing with the portion of the passage this study emphasizes (as discussed in Chapter 2).

*[ὄντας ὑμᾶς] [God made Gentile believers alive together with Christ, raised them together with Christ, and seated them together with Christ],[23] even though they were spiritually dead in their trespasses and sins (2:1).

Some commentators consider the chapter division here unfortunate at best.[24] Denbow even goes so far as to suggest that ὑμᾶς is the second direct object of ἐγείρας in

---

[20] E.g., the unit of text might be a dependent clause, adverbial prepositional phrase, etc. See Appendix 1 for details.

[21] In this context, *topic* is a technical term referring to the entire proposition which the dependent text modifies.

[22] Under the BAR method, an exegete begins outlining from the bottom (i.e., the details of the text) and work upward to main points. The presentation in this thesis mirrors the inductive process of exegesis under that method (see Appendix 1 for details). The bottom-level outline statements appear in the full outline at the E level in verses 1–7 and at the D level in verses 8–10 (see the full outline in Appendix 2). Those who prefer a more deductive presentation may refer to Appendix 2 before continuing.

[23] Information in brackets here derives from 2:5b–6.

[24] Max Turner, "Ephesians," in *New Bible Commentary*, 4th ed., edited by G. J. Wenham, J. A. Motyer, D. A. Carson, and R. T. France (Leicester and Downers Grove, IL: Inter-Varsity, 1994), 1228; Archibald M. Hunter, *Galatians, Ephesians, Philippians, Colossians*, Layman's Bible Commentary, ed. Balmer H. Kelly, vol. 22 (Richmond, VA: Knox, 1959), 52–54.

1:20.[25] These commentators do have a point: Paul's argument in 2:1–10 does have a direct, organic relationship to the preceding paragraph, 1:15–23. As Darby expresses it,

> . . . the work which has been wrought in Christ, and the display of the power of God, which took place in raising Him from the grave to the right hand of God the Father above every name that is named, are the expression and model of the action of the same power which works in us who believe, which has raised us from our state of death in sin to have part in the glory of this same Christ.[26]

However, the close connection is semantic, not grammatical, in nature. Denbow has missed the internal cohesion of the sentence in 2:1–7. The parallel structure of the concessive participial clauses here and in 2:5a requires that this be a separate sentence, because the καὶ of 2:5 links them, and they jointly attach to a distinct core proposition in 2:5b–6. Best observes that Denbow's linkage with 1:15–23 may present other problems as well: "Quite apart from the way in which this makes 1.20b–23 parenthetical, Denbow's solution makes the death of Christ parallel to that of believers, i.e. a death in trespasses and sins."[27]

The identity of the two pronouns ὑμᾶς and ἡμᾶς in Ephesians 1–2 is prerequisite to rightly understanding of the doctrinal section. The contrast initially appears in 1:11–14, where Paul not only sets apart two groups of people with distinguishing characteristics (*we who first trusted . . .* and *you also*), but verse 14 also gives parallel ideas: *you* were

---

[25] Walter H. Denbow, "A Note on *Ephesians* II. I." *Congregational Quarterly* 35 (January 1957): 62–24.

[26] J. N. Darby, *Synopsis of the Books of the Bible*, vol. 4, *Acts–Philippians* (New York: Loizeaux, n.d.; reprint, Oak Park, IL: Bible Truth, 1970), 392. For further discussion of the relationship between 1:15–23 and 2:1–10, see the paragraph-level statement on page 38.

[27] Ernest Best, "Dead in Trespasses and Sins (Eph. 2.1)," in *Essays on Ephesians* (Edinburgh: Clark, 1997), 77, n. 43.

sealed with the Spirit, who is also the guarantee of *our* inheritance. From 1:11–14 alone, one only knows that the salvation of the *we* group occurred before it happened for the *you* group. Ephesians 2:11–13 and 3:1–13 explicitly identify the *you* group as Gentiles.[28] Since the *we* group was saved first, and then the *you* group, one must ask, "Which group of people came to Christ before the Gentiles?" There can be only one answer: the Jews.[29] Beginning in 1:13–14 and continuing in 2:1–10, Paul lays the doctrinal groundwork for uniting these two disparate groups into one entity.

The participle ὄντας modifies the main verbs in 2:5b–6. Paul here addresses the Gentile believers' former estate. They were spiritually dead in their trespasses and sins. The idea here is concessive: despite their dead state, He saved them.

[ποτε περιεπατήσατε] **The manner in which the Gentile believers formerly lived was in sin according to this world and according to Satan, who works in the disobedient (that is, in unbelievers) (2:2).**

Gentile believers were not only spiritually dead, Paul says, but they were wallowing in the filth associated with their state. They lived in a worldly manner, in fact in a satanic manner. The identity of τοῖς υἱοῖς τῆς ἀπειθείας (*the sons of disobedience*) as unbelievers is hardly in doubt here, given the positional nature of the discussion and the fact that they are clearly distinguished from both Gentile believers and Jewish

---

[28] Naturally *you* refers particularly to the Ephesian audience of the letter, but these passages clarify that Paul is not writing to the Ephesians *qua* audience only, but to the Ephesians *qua* Gentile believers.

[29] Recall that not until Acts 10 (the conversion of Cornelius) are Gentiles *qua* Gentiles included in the church. Proselytes, ethnic Gentiles converted to Judaism, were considered Jews in this regard.

believers.³⁰ Paul also uses the same phrase again in 5:5–7. In that context, Paul does not refer to sinning believers: he urges the Ephesian believers not to partake with the sons of disobedience, again distinguishing them as a separate group destined for God's wrath.

[καὶ ἡμεῖς ... ποτε] Jewish believers also formerly lived among [the disobedient] (2:3a).

The antecedent of οἷς is the sons of disobedience in the preceding clause. Jewish believers lived among the unbelieving targets of God's wrath. Paul's use of πάντες here emphatically places himself as part of this group: this discussion applies even to "good" Jews like him.³¹

[ἐν ... ποιοῦντες] The manner in which [Jewish believers formerly lived among the disobedient] was in their flesh's passions, doing the flesh's and the mind's desires (2:3b).

The preceding statement (2:3a) was no pious Jew's lament at the depravity that surrounded his holy (if unbelieving) former life. Rather, Paul says, the Jewish believers not only formerly lived among the disobedient; they lived in accordance with their fleshly urges in a manner essentially indistinguishable from their neighbors.

[και] In addition to [living in a fleshly manner among the disobedient], Jewish believers were also (then) by nature recipients of (divine) wrath, just like the rest (of the disobedient) (2:3c).

One might suppose, given their manner of life, that the Jewish believers were formerly targets of God's wrath because of their conduct. That manner of life does

---

³⁰ Note that ποτε and νῦν in 2:2 contrast *the sons of disobedience* to the Gentile believers, and in 2:3, ἐν οἷς contrasts them to the Jewish believers.

³¹ Cf. Phil. 3:4–6.

indeed call down wrath on all participants, believer and unbeliever alike, as Paul says later in 5:5–7. However, Paul does not seek to make that point here. Here he says that they were children of wrath not through their conduct, but by their very *nature*, further reinforcing the conception of death in the passage as spiritual, positional, and forensic rather than merely existential and behavioral.

*[Θεὸς] God [made Gentile believers and Jewish believers alive together with Christ, raised them together with Christ, and seated them together with Christ] (2:4a).

Θεὸς is the grammatical subject of the sentence. Having introduced the objects of the salvation of which he will speak, Paul now turns his attention to the subject, the One who saves. The remainder of the paragraph will focus on God and His agenda in salvation.

[ὤν] The reason [God made Gentile believers and Jewish believers alive together with Christ, raised them together with Christ, and seated them together with Christ] is because He is rich in mercy (2:4a).

Before moving on to his main point, Paul lays out the beginnings of the reason why God would save people like those he has just described in 2:1–3. The description Paul has given of the Gentile and Jewish objects of salvation fairly cries out for judgment. Lifting such people to the dizzying heights of the salvation he is about to describe calls for some explanation. At this point he could simply have said, "God is merciful." But having made a point of the monstrous nature of the believers' former life, Paul now wishes to make a point of the greatness of God's mercy. This is in sharp contrast to the objects of salvation: as they are great in iniquity, so God is *rich* in mercy. His reservoir is more than adequate to the great needs of sinners.

[διὰ] The reason [God is rich in mercy] is because He loved Jewish (and Gentile) believers (2:4b).

The identity of *us* is an issue here. Of course many see every second-person usage in 2:1–10 as a reference to all believers. However, even many of those who see *we* in 2:3 as referring exclusively to Jewish believers see *us* here (and in 2:5a, 7) as pointing to all believers.[32] However, while it is theologically true that God's love for all believers motivated his saving mercy on them, one must question whether that is what Paul is expressing here. Paul has (in 1:13–14) placed Jewish and Gentile believers on parallel tracks, noting that they share a common Savior and a common security. But in the passages where he contrasts first- and second-person pronouns, he has not yet joined Jewish and Gentile believers into one group. The common ground has been discussed briefly, but the inference of unity has yet to be drawn. Therefore, a reader at this point in the book must interpret the second person in a way that is consistent with its usage thus far. So why the parenthetical reference to Gentile believers in the outline statement? Paul does not directly address God's love for Gentiles in this verse, but his inclusion of them as objects of salvation justifies the inference that God loved them as well.[33] Thus, as Paul earlier portrayed the Gentiles as lately included in the going concern of Jewish salvation,[34] now he portrays them as objects of a salvation motivated by God's love for

---

[32] See further discussion on pages 46–49.

[33] Thus the difference between the inclusive and exclusive interpretations of *us* lies in whether the outline statement encloses *Gentiles* in parentheses, or not: "Jewish (and Gentile) believers" *versus* "Jewish and Gentile believers."

[34] See 1:12–13.

the Jews. Once again, "salvation is of the Jews." A particular strength to this view is the fact that the upcoming *we* in 2:5a refers to Jewish believers exclusively.[35]

*[καὶ ὄντας] [God made Jewish believers alive together with Christ, raised them together with Christ, and seated them together with Christ] although they were spiritually dead in sins (2:5a).

This construction runs parallel to 2:1, making the same point regarding the Jewish believers. The discussion of believers' former state follows a chiastic structure briefly interrupted by 2:4, thus:

A. The Gentile believers were formerly spiritually dead (2:1).

    B. The abhorrent manner of Gentile believers' former life (2:2).

    B´. The equally abhorrent manner of Jewish believers' former life (2:3).

A´. The Jewish believers were formerly spiritually dead (2:5a).

The placement of A´ after 2:4 only underscores the depth of God's love and mercy.

*[συνεζωοποίησεν … καὶ συνήγειρεν καὶ συνεκάθισεν] God made Jewish and Gentile believers alive together with Christ, raised them together with Christ, and seated them in the heavens together with Christ, that is, He saved Gentile (and Jewish) believers by grace (2:5b–6).

Here are the three main verbs of the sentence. The συν- prefix does not directly join Jews and Gentiles together, but in conjunction with τῷ Χριστῷ indicates union with Christ. The joining of Jews and Gentiles derives grammatically from the implicit direct objects together with the nature of the verbs: in that both groups share a common salvation through union with Christ, they are inevitably united to each other.[36] Paul's

---

[35] In parallel with the exclusively Gentile ὑμᾶς in 2:1.

[36] A point Paul will make at some length in 2:11–22.

exposition of their union with Christ here corresponds to his prayer in 1:19–21.[37] There, Paul asks that God grant the Ephesians knowledge of how great His power is toward believers. Specifically, Paul compares the magnitude of the Father's working in believers to the manner in which He worked in Christ, ἐγείρας αὐτὸν ἐκ τῶν νεκρῶν καὶ ἐκάθισεν ἐν δεξιᾷ αὐτοῦ ἐν τοῖς ἐπουρανίοις (*raising Him from among the dead, and He seated Him on His right hand in the heavenlies*). Christ was raised; so also were believers corporately raised with Christ. Christ was seated in the heavenlies; believers were corporately seated with Him. What the Father has done for the Head, He has done also for the Body.

The parenthetical comment χάριτί ἐστε σεσῳσμένοι (*by grace you are saved*) does not grammatically connect to anything else in this sentence: Paul assures that the readers will notice the disjunction by changing the person and number of the verb. The subject of *by grace you are saved*, an implicit ὑμεῖς, refers directly to the Ephesian Gentile audience. However, the truth herein stated applies implicitly to the Jewish believers also, since they too were dead in sins (thus undeserving of God's favor) and are now united together with Christ in the same manner as the Gentile believers. The grammatically connected portions of the sentence address the situation from the point of view of its grammatical subject, *God*, while the parenthesis, by shifting its subject to *you*, addresses the same situation from man's point of view. Thus *by grace you are saved*

---

[37] This point has been noted in the literature. See Thomas G. Allen, "Exaltation and Solidarity with Christ: Ephesians 1.20 and 2.6," *Journal for the Study of the New Testament* 28 (October 1986): 103–20.

functions as a succinct summary of Paul's thought in the sentence to this point, viewed from a different angle (see table below).

And you, being dead in trespasses and sins, among which you once walked according to the age of this world, according to the prince of the power of the air, the spirit now working in the sons of disobedience among whom we all also formerly conducted ourselves in the lusts of our flesh, doing the will of the flesh and of the mind, and were by nature children of wrath, as *were* also the rest . . . us also being dead in sin	by grace . . .
but God . . . made *you and us* alive together with Christ—by grace you are saved—and raised *you and us* together and seated *you and us* together in the heavenlies in Christ	. . .you are saved

[ἵνα] The purpose for [God saving believers by grace] was in order that He might display the overwhelming abundance of His grace in the coming ages by means of His kindness to believers (2:7).

Paul here reveals God's purpose for by-grace salvation: to demonstrate His grace. That God would take the former children of wrath and be kind to them, uniting them with Christ, with all that entails, will be His unparalleled monument to the abundance of His grace. Paul will return to this thought in 2:9–10.

*[χάριτί ἐστε σεσῳσμένοι] [God] saved believers by grace (2:8a).

The phrase *by grace you are saved* parenthetically summarizes the three main verbs of the preceding sentence. Paul re-introduces his continuing theme here at the beginning of the sentence, with two differences in wording. The signpost γὰρ (*for*) that connects 2:8–9 to the preceding sentence indicates a further explanation of Paul's theme, and makes explicit the relation between the two sentences. The addition of the article τῇ is often considered anaphoric, referring back to the preceding uses of χάρις (*grace*) in 2:5 and 2:7,[38] but a better explanation exists.[39]

*[διὰ] The means by which [believers are saved by grace] is through faith (2:8a)

Grace is the motive power behind salvation, as Paul has already made abundantly clear. God saves by grace, in order to display His grace. The addition of *through faith* here takes nothing from the grace of God. Faith is the instrument by which the saving grace of God is applied to a given individual. In philosophical terms, grace is the principal cause of salvation, and faith is the instrumental cause.[40] If grace is to salvation as electricity is to a light bulb, faith is the light switch.

*[καὶ τοῦτο] The implication of [salvation being by means of grace] is that salvation is not (accomplished) by man, but rather it is a gift from God, not something obtained through work (2:8b–9a).

With respect to this portion of the sentence, the import of the predicate is rarely debated: *something* is not accomplished by man, but is a gift of God, not obtained through works. A child could understand it—many do. But *what* is the subject of discussion? Here debate rages, centering around a seemingly simple grammatical question: what is the antecedent of τοῦτο (*this*)? Chapter 6 will take up the question in

---

[38] E.g., Harold W. Hoehner, *Ephesians: An Exegetical Commentary* (Grand Rapids: Baker Academic, 2002), 340; Andrew T. Lincoln, *Ephesians*, Word Biblical Commentary, ed. David A. Hubbard and Glenn W. Barker; New Testament, ed. Ralph P. Martin, vol. 42 (Dallas: Word, 1990), 111. This idea has found a comfortable home in more homiletical expositions of the passage as well, e.g., Jim Townsend, "'Saved by Grace Alone—This is All my Plea' (An Exposition of Ephesians 2:8–10)," *Emmaus Journal* 7 (Winter 1998); electronic reprint (Garland, TX: Galaxie, 2002), 230–40.

[39] See pages 64–65.

[40] This particular issue is one of the seven deferred to the next chapter. See pages 65–67.

detail, but for now a summary will suffice. Neuter forms of οὗτος (the near demonstrative pronoun, *this, these*) in the Pauline corpus generally refer to a conceptual (i.e., multiple-word) antecedent, and rarely, perhaps never[41] to a single-word feminine antecedent, which renders πίστεως (*faith*) and χάριτι (*grace*) unlikely at best. A few suggest that καὶ τοῦτο should be translated *and especially*, but this is untenable. There is little textual support (none whatever in the Pauline corpus) for the idea that τοῦτο loses its pronominal force in that construction. The likelihood of the solution discussed below makes resort to such an arcane interpretation highly suspect. Finally, some have argued that χάριτί ἐστε σεσῳσμένοι διὰ τῆς πίστεως (*by grace you are saved through faith*) should be the referent. This is closer to the truth, but upon further examination διὰ τῆς πίστεως (*through faith*) is not part of the referent. The topic throughout the passage is χάριτί ἐστε σεσῳσμένοι (*by grace you are saved*), which summarizes the main verbs of 2:5–6 and is repeated in 2:8. This key concept, by-grace salvation, is the referent of τοῦτο. By-grace salvation does not come from its objects, rather, it is the gift of God, and not obtained by works.

[ἵνα μη] The purpose of [by-grace salvation being a gift] is in order that no one can boast (2:9b).

In keeping with God's purpose to display His grace through salvation, no boasting by man can be admitted. Grace can be demonstrated only if the salvation it achieves is a gift, and if a gift, the recipient has no room for claiming credit. Christendom has often been less than clear on this point, so it bears some amplification. Salvation as a reward

---

[41] 2 Cor. 13:9 and Phil. 1:28 are arguable, although in each case a conceptual (multiple-word) antecedent is available. See discussion page 83, n. 18.

for the past or current deeds, however trivial, of the recipient, would be a good deal, but not a gift, and might admit some modicum of human boasting. Salvation as a loan, collateralized by the future good deeds, however trivial, of the recipient, would be a good deal, but not a gift, and might admit some modicum of human boasting. But by making salvation a gift contingent on neither past, nor present, nor future works of any kind, God has outflanked man. Eternity will ring with boasting about salvation—but the boasting will be God's, and God's alone.

*[γάρ] The reason [by-grace salvation is God's gift, which precludes human boasting] is because believers are corporately God's creation (2:10a).

The signpost γάρ indicates that Paul is further explaining his point: this by-grace salvation precludes boasting because it is a work done by God. Why is this true? Because *we are His artifact*. The plural verb ἐσμεν (*are*) links an implicit plural subject, ὑμεῖς (*we*), with the singular predicate nominative ποίημα (*artifact, creation,* or *work*). Thus this passage does not speak of each believer as a divinely-made individual, but of believers corporately as His single work. Paul previously hinted at this idea in 1:23, introducing the church as Christ's body, and again in 2:1–7, where he implies the union of Jewish and Gentile believers through their co-union with Christ. He will develop the concept of corporate identity further as he progresses through the book.

[κτισθέντες] The reason [believers are corporately God's creation] is because God created them in Christ Jesus (2:10b).

The participle here fleshes out the concept of corporate identity: God *created* the single artifact of which both Jewish and Gentile believers are a part. The phrase ἐν Χριστῷ Ἰησοῦ (*in Christ Jesus*) links the corporate identity concept to the numerous occurrences of *in Christ* in Ephesians.[42] The meaning of the concept is hotly debated, and since it is incidental to the argument of this thesis, it will not be addressed here.

[ἐπὶ] The purpose [for God making believers into a single, corporate creation] is in order that they [corporately] might do good works (10b).

The discussion here revolves around the church as God's singular creation: He made the church in order to do good works. This is entirely in accord with the purpose expressed in 2:7. What would make a better trophy for God's grace than people who were formerly vile sinners, relishing their wickedness, but now are made into a corporate entity that not only is saved from spiritual death, but participates in the good works?[43]

[προητοίμασεν] God prepared [the good works believers are to do] beforehand in order that believers [corporately] should walk in them (2:10c).

God is not improvising the destiny of His trophy. He has planned the destiny of His church, not only for what it will *be*, which he has previously discussed in 1:3–14, but also for what it (collectively) will *do*.

Upper-Level Outline Statements

This presentation of the upper-level points will proceed by sentence, first considering all upper-level points for the first sentence (2:1–7), then proceeding to

---

[42] The concept appears in various permutations of language: "in Christ," "in Him," "in Whom," "in the Lord," etc. See Hoehner, *Ephesians*, 173–74; Clarence B. Hale, *The Meaning of "In Christ" in the Greek New Testament* (Dallas: SIL, 1991), 26–36, for the occurrences in Ephesians.

[43] Note that this passage does not support perseverance of the saints with respect to experiential sanctification. Such an interpretation fails to understand the corporate focus of the book. Paul uses the interwoven themes of the mystery, the body image, the building image, and the *one new man*, among others, to reinforce this focus. See John H. Niemelä, "*If Anyone's Work Is Burned*: Scrutinizing Proof-Texts," *CTS Journal* 8 (January–March 2002): 22–42, for further discussion of Ephesians 2:1–10 in particular.

consider each of the remaining sentences in turn. As above, the outline statements will appear in boldface type, followed by commentary in plain text.

[God saved Jewish and Gentile believers by grace] although the Gentile believers were (once) spiritually dead and lived in a worldly and satanic manner, and Jewish believers also formerly lived among unbelievers in a fleshly manner, and were under God's wrath because of their sinful nature, just like the Gentile believers were (2:1–3).

This statement draws together the five bottom-level statements for 2:1–3.[44] In three verses Paul introduces the objects of the salvation he is about to discuss, and encapsulates the lost estate from which they come: spiritual death. Moreover, the believers' former manner of life cannot be described as some sort of noble paganism: Paul says they all, Gentile and Jew alike, lived in a manner fully consonant with their dead state.

God made both Jewish and Gentile believers alive together with Christ, and raised them together with Christ, and seated them together with Christ, that is, He saved them by grace, because His great love causes Him to be merciful, in order that He might display His grace (2:4–7).

The six remaining outline statements for the sentence come together in this statement.[45] The reader now encounters the main clause, which discusses God's saving activity for Jewish and Gentile believers. He does this by uniting them with Christ. Christ is alive, thus they too are alive; Christ is raised, thus they too are raised; Christ is seated in the heavenlies, thus they too are seated with Him: this is being saved by grace. God does this out of mercy motivated by His great love, in order to display His grace.

---

[44] These statements appear on pages 23–26 and in Appendix 2.

[45] These statements appear on pages 27–31 and in Appendix 2.

God made both Jewish and Gentile believers alive together with Christ, and raised them together with Christ, and seated them together with Christ, that is, He saved them by grace (even though both were dead in their sins and under His wrath), because of His love-motivated mercy, in order that He might display His grace (2:1–7).

This statement brings together the two halves of the sentence into a single coherent whole. The order differs from that of the text, because the subject and main verbs appear first. Paraphrase and rearrangement allow the exegete to portray the interpretation with maximum clarity. However, the statement represents all the content of 2:1–7, albeit in summary form.

[γὰρ] In light of [God saving believers by grace in order to display grace], the means by which believers are saved by grace is through faith, and as a result salvation is not accomplished by man but given by God, in order that no one be able to boast about being saved by grace (2:8–9).

This statement summarizes the four D-level points for the second sentence of the paragraph.[46] Having presented his theme (by-grace salvation), Paul now expands on it: it is obtained through faith. Moreover, by-grace salvation is a gift, not in any way to be acquired through man's work. Giving salvation in this way precludes all human boasting and therefore allows God the fullest possible latitude for accomplishing His stated purpose in the endeavor: the demonstration of His grace. Indeed, there is no other way to demonstrate grace except on those who have not earned it, who have no claim on its benefits. Salvation is *not of works*, but what good work could the wretched people described in 2:1-3 do? In large measure, 2:8–9 merely renders explicit what was already implicit in 2:1–7.

---

[46] These points appear on pages 31–33 and in Appendix 2.

The reason [no one can boast about being saved by grace] is because believers are corporately God's creation because He made them in Christ for the purpose of doing the good works that He prepared for them beforehand (2:10).

The four D-level points of 2:10 come together in this statement.[47] When God, in the ages to come, wishes to show someone the glory of His grace, to what will He point? What is his trophy? Here Paul tells us: it is the church, God's *magnum opus* which He made for the purpose of executing His preplanned good works.

Based on [his just-completed prayer that God will reveal to the Ephesians the greatness of His power that works in them (the power that raised Christ from the dead and seated Him in the heavenlies)],[48] Paul explains that God made Jewish and Gentile believers alive together with Christ, and raised them together with Christ, and seated them together with Christ, that is, He saved them by grace (even though they were both spiritually dead and were living accordingly, and were both under His wrath) because of His love-motivated mercy, in order that He might display His grace, and the means by which they were saved by grace is through faith, and by implication, by-grace salvation is God's work and man cannot boast about it, because God created the church as His corporate (singular) creation in Christ for the purpose of doing the good works that He prepared for it (2:1–10).

This statement takes the statements for the three sentences (2:1–7, 2:8–9, and 2:10) and builds them into one coherent statement that preserves the argument of the paragraph. The statement is a single (run-on) sentence, as BAR statements always are. The single-sentence format forces the exegete to articulate the nature of the relations between all parts of the paragraph, including those across the sentence breaks in the text.[49] The statement also articulates the meaning of the paragraph in relation to the paragraph that precedes it. As mentioned above, certain commentators correctly note that

---

[47] See pages 34–35 or Appendix 2.

[48] 1:15–23.

[49] See Appendix 1 for more information.

the relationship between 1:15–23 and 2:1–10 is quite close. MacDonald expresses the connection well:

> The chapter break should not obscure the vital connection between the latter part of chapter 1 and the verses that follow. There we watched the mighty power of God as it raised Christ from the grave and crowned Him with glory and honor. Now we see how that same power has worked in our own lives, raising us from spiritual death and seating us in the heavenlies.[50]

MacDonald might have added that in 1:15–23 Paul prays that God would grant his Ephesian readers understanding of three things, the last of which is the greatness of God's power toward believers—which power raised and exalted Christ. Having asked God's blessing on his teaching efforts, Paul proceeds to explain just how that power works in believers: they are identified with Christ, and therefore made alive, raised, and seated with Him, that is, saved by grace.

FOLLOWING CONTEXT

Having explained that Jewish and Gentile believers formerly had a common spiritual problem (death) and share a common deliverance through union with Christ, Paul goes on to explain the implications of their union with Christ. Although Gentile believers were formerly far from God, while Jews were near, that distinction has now been erased, and the two are joined into one new man, so that through the Holy Spirit they both now have access to God. Gentile believers are now joined inseparably with Jewish believers, and together God is making them into a temple for Him.

---

[50] William MacDonald, *Believer's Bible Commentary: Old and New Testaments*, ed. Art Farstad (Nashville, TN: Nelson, 1995), 1915.

Paul opens his second prayer at this point, but makes an aside to explain the phrase "prisoner of Christ for you Gentiles." Concerned that his readers will be disheartened that they are the cause of his trials, Paul explains that God has given him a particular ministry: proclaiming the mystery (that Gentile believers are fellow inheritors, one body, and fellow partakers of the promises with Jewish believers), to the Gentiles. Therefore, his readers are not to be disheartened, because ministry to them is God's grace given to Paul, and accordingly his sufferings are their glory. Paul then continues his prayer, asking that God strengthen his readers in order that Christ dwell in their hearts, as a result of which they might come to comprehend the dimensions of Christ's knowledge-surpassing love, which will enable them to be filled with God's fullness. Paul closes the doctrinal section with a doxological prayer that Almighty God be glorified in the church.

The first paragraph in the practical section, 4:1–6, is the kernel of the book of Ephesians. In these six short verses, Paul summarizes the preceding three chapters and gives the overriding command of which 4:7–6:20 is a detailed exposition: walk worthy of the church's calling. The worthy walk is dedicated to humility and unity, because of the nature of the calling itself: believers are called into a single, unified body with a unified destiny by a unified Godhead, who rules everything, moves everything, and indwells them.

CHAPTER 4

HIGHLIGHTS FROM THE INTERPRETIVE TRADITION

INTRODUCION

As mentioned in the Introduction, seven particular points of data in Ephesians 2:1–10 inform the theological argument of this study. The first six are composed of three pairs of issues: the meanings of (1) *you* and (2) *we*, the meanings of (3) *dead* and (4) *made alive*, and the relation of and *by grace you are saved* to its contexts (5) in 2:5 and (6) in 2:8. The seventh issue is the relation of *through faith* to its context. Note that all seven points are drawn from the emphasized text of the passage (i.e., the core propositions, nonverbal modifiers, or concessive clauses) as discussed in Chapter 2.[1] This chapter will survey the commentary literature on these seven points, considering each of the paired issues together, then the seventh issue by itself.

MEANING OF *YOU* AND *WE*

There are a total of six available positions (which this study will designate with the letters *A–F*) regarding the meaning of *you* and *we*. Five of these positions (A–E) recognize some degree of distinction between the pronouns. The sixth position, F, does not recognize any difference between *you* and *we* in this passage. Among those who distinguish between *you* and *we* in the passage, there are two interpretive options for each pronoun. *You* refers to the Ephesian believers in any case, but is Paul referring to them as not-Paul, i.e., as his audience, or as Gentile believers? On the other hand, *we* refers either

---

[1] See pages 9–18.

to all believers or exclusively to Jewish believers. The combination of options yields a two by two grid that charts positions A–D, as below.[2]

Positions on *You* and *We*

	We = all believers	*We* = Jewish believers
You = audience	A	B
You = Gentile believers	C	D

Position A

Lincoln explains position A:

> ... the distinction between *you* and *we* is not intended to be one between Gentile and Jew so much as one between the readers in particular and Christians in general, including the writer.... What is said about those referred to as "we all" in v 3 is not something distinctive to Jews rather than Gentiles, and it becomes clear from the rest of the pericope that the Gentile-Jew distinction cannot be maintained consistently. The *we* who were dead through trespasses in v 5a are not Jews as opposed to Gentiles who were dead through trespasses in v 1.... The continuation of the first person plural in vv 4, 5a, 7, 10 is the style of confessional material, which allows for a broad reference to all believers ... and the interchange

---

[2] Position B seems to be purely hypothetical. It makes little sense that Paul would discuss Jewish believers in terms of their race, but then turn to discussing the Ephesians *qua* audience, and leave the subject of the Gentile believers as a class untouched.

between the *you* and the *we* style has the force of making the readers feel included in the church as a whole.[3]

Bloomfield seems to hold the same view, although he does note the racial composition of the Ephesian church.[4] Best also notes the racial composition, but makes his support of Position A quite clear.[5] Hoehner now agrees: "The contrast Paul is making is thought by some to be between Paul as a Jew and the Ephesians as Gentiles, but more likely it is between him as writer and the Ephesians as recipients."[6] His earlier work is unclear about the identity of "you," seemingly making no distinction in 2:1, and not clearly differentiating between the Ephesians *qua* Gentiles and the Ephesians *qua* audience in his discussion of 2:3.[7]

Calvin suffers from a similar lack of clarity regarding the distinction between Ephesians *qua* Gentiles and the Ephesians *qua* audience, but unfortunately does not resolve it:

---

[3] Andrew T. Lincoln, *Ephesians*, Word Biblical Commentary, ed. David A. Hubbard and Glenn W. Barker; New Testament, ed. Ralph P. Martin, vol. 42 (Dallas: Word, 1990), 88.

[4] S. T. Bloomfield, Ἡ Καινη Διαθηκη. *The Greek Testament with English Notes, Critical, Philological, and Exegetical*, 2nd ed., vol. 2 (London: n.p., n.d.; reprint, Philadelphia: Lippincott, 1860), 266.

[5] Ernest Best, *A Critical and Exegetical Commentary on Ephesians*, International Critical Commentary on the Holy Scriptures of the Old and New Testaments (Edinburgh: Clark, 1998), 199, 207–8. Best commendably addresses pronoun consistency issues in the book, referring back to 1:3–14 to bolster his position. Unfortunately he does not see that Paul there argues that Gentile believers should bless God because He planned, executed and guarantees the salvation of the Jewish believers—a salvation in which the Gentile believers also fully participate (a consistent Position D approach).

[6] Harold W. Hoehner, *Ephesians: An Exegetical Commentary* (Grand Rapids: Baker Academic, 2002), 317.

[7] Harold W. Hoehner, "Ephesians," in *The Bible Knowledge Commentary*, ed. John F. Walvoord and Roy B. Zuck, vol. 2, *New Testament* (Wheaton, IL: Victor, 1983), 622, "Unregenerate persons are dead" (regarding 2:1) *versus* "**All of us also lived among them at one time** is Paul's reminder to his Gentile readers that the Jews ('all of us') also joined in this disobedience." The space limitations inherent in the *Bible Knowledge Commentary* format may underlie the lack of clarity.

> Lest it should be supposed that what he had now said was a slanderous reproach against the former character of the Ephesians, or that Jewish pride had led him to treat the Gentiles as an inferior race, he associates himself and his countrymen along with them in the general accusation. This is not done in hypocrisy, but in a sincere ascription of glory to God.[8]

From his comments on 2:5a, however, it is clear that Calvin does maintain an inclusive view of *we* in that passage:

> *Even when we were dead in sin.* These words have the same emphasis as similar expressions in another Epistle.
> "For *when we were yet without strength,* in due time Christ died, for the ungodly. — But God commendeth his love toward us, in that, *while we were yet sinners,* Christ died for us."
> (Romans 5:6, 8.)[9]

Consequently, Calvin is difficult to classify. It seems that he holds Position A, but he may hold position C or even E.

Position C

Positions A and C agree about *we*, (inclusive of all believers), but disagree about *you*. Rather than seeing *you* as a reference to the Ephesians *qua* audience, position C views *you* as referring to the Ephesians *qua* Gentiles. As Perkins succinctly states it, "The section shifts from the Gentile past of the letter's audience, 'you,' to the experience of salvation shared by all Christians, 'we.'"[10] Jamieson, Fausset, and Brown hold this

---

[8]John Calvin, *Commentaries on the Epistles of Paul to the Galatians and Ephesians*, trans. William Pringle (Edinburgh: Calvin Translation Society, n.d.; reprint, Grand Rapids: Baker, 1981), 222.

[9] Calvin, *Galatians and Ephesians*, 225.

[10] Pheme Perkins, "Ephesians," in *2 Corinthians–Philemon*, New Interpreter's Bible, ed. Leander E. Keck, et al., vol. 11 (Nashville: Abingdon, 2000), 388–89.

position, albeit tentatively.[11] Also among this group are Salmond and Alford,[12] who both argue that the *we all* of 2:3 requires an inclusive view. Salmond's reasoning rests on Paul's theological propensities:

> Paul seldom misses the opportunity of declaring the universal sinfulness of men, the dire level of corruptness on which all, however they differed in race or privilege, stood. So here ἡμεῖς πάντες is best taken in its utmost breadth—not merely "all the Jewish-Christians" . . . but = the whole body of us Christians, Jewish and Gentile alike included.[13]

Salmond fails to notice, however, that the most restrictive definition of *we* (Jewish believers) still allows Paul "the opportunity of declaring the universal sinfulness of men," since the collected statements "you were dead" (v. 1) and "we were dead" (2:5) exclude no one in any case.[14] Alford's argumentation is more exegetical:

> The usage of ἡμεῖς πάντες by St. Paul must decide. It occurs Rom. iv. 16, ὅς ἐστιν πατὴρ πάντων ἡμῶν, undeniably for Jews and Gentiles included (for the slight difference arising from πάντων being first, and therefore emphatic, need not be insisted on): viii. 32, ὑπὲρ ἡμῶν πάντων παρέδωκεν αὐτόν, where the universal reference is as undeniable: 1 Cor. xii. 13, where it is still more marked: ἡμεῖς πάντες. . . . εἴτε Ἰουδαῖοι εἴτε Ἕλληνες εἴτε δοῦλοι εἴτε ἐλεύθεροι: 2 Cor. iii. 18, equally undoubted. It can hardly be then that here he should have departed from his universal usage, and placed an unmeaning πάντες after ἡμεῖς merely to signify, 'we Jews, every one of us.' I therefore infer that by ἡμεῖς πάντες, he means, we all, Jews and Gentiles alike . . .[15]

---

[11] Robert Jamieson, A. R. Fausset, and David Brown, *Commentary Practical and Explanatory on the Whole Bible*, rev. ed. (Grand Rapids: Zondervan, 1961), 1283.

[12] S. D. F. Salmond, "The Epistle to the Ephesians," in *The Expositor's Greek New Testament*, ed. W. Robertson Nicoll, vol. 3 (Grand Rapids: Eerdmans, 1961), 285; Henry F. Alford, *The Greek New Testament*, vol. 3, *Galatians–Philemon*, rev. Everett F. Harrison (Chicago: Moody Press, 1968), 88, 90.

[13] Salmond, "Ephesians," 285.

[14] See further discussion under Position D, page 49.

[15] Alford, *Greek New Testament*, 90.

One could add 2 Cor. 5:10 and Gal. 4:26 to Alford's list. Alford is quite correct that nowhere outside Ephesians does Paul use "we all" in an exclusive sense, but he makes two serious errors. First, he commits illegitimate totality transfer, which Barr defines as

> The error that arises, when the 'meaning' of a word (understood as the total series of relations in which it is used in the literature) is read into a particular case as its sense and implication there, may be called 'illegitimate totality transfer'.[16]

Alford would be guilty of illegitimate totality transfer even if the language at issue were something more specific, but he compounds the error by applying the fallacy to verbiage as blatantly context-dependent as *we all*. Surely one cannot confer the status of technical terminology on such a generic expression. The Ephesian readers could not refer to the Roman or Corinthian letters in order to determine Paul's intent in 2:3; they had no choice but to make sense of it based on its immediate context. Modern readers should be so wise.

A Mediate Position (E)

A popular position straddles the line between positions C and D, agreeing with position C in 2:4–7, but with D in 2:3, as the chart on page 47 shows. Markus Barth explains: "In vss. 1–3 the pronouns *you* and *we* denoted Gentiles and Jews respectively. In vss. 4–5 the pronouns *us* and *we* describe in hymnic form the saints of Jewish *and* Gentile origin as a community."[17]

---

[16] James Barr, *The Semantics of Biblical Language* (London: Oxford, 1961; reprint, London: SCM, 1987), 218.

[17] Markus Barth, *Ephesians: Introduction, Translation, and Commentary on Chapters 1–3*, The Anchor Bible, ed. William Foxwell Albright and David Noel Freedman, vol. 34 (Garden City, NY: Doubleday, 1974), 219.

Positions on *You* and *We*

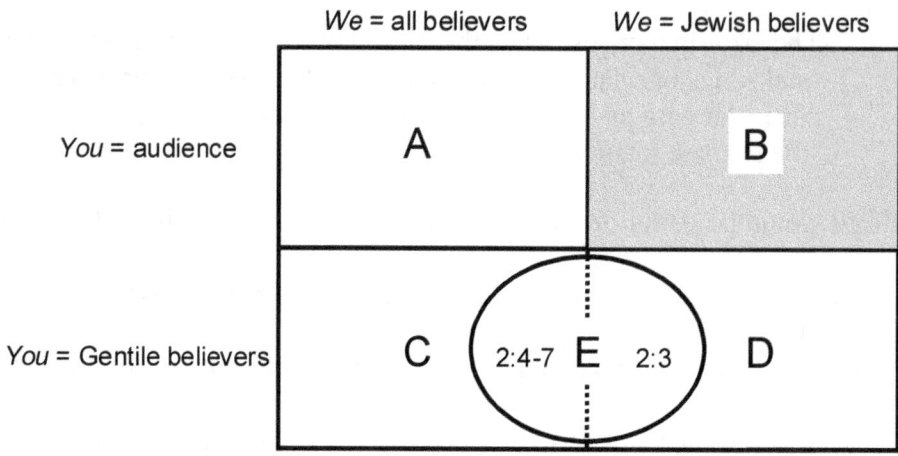

Braune, Eadie, Barclay, Beare and Wedel, Darby, Simpson, Gill, Hunter, MacDonald, Hughes, and Ralph P. Martin agree, as does F. F. Bruce, if more tentatively.[18] Alfred

---

[18] Karl Braune, *The Epistle of Paul to the Ephesians*, trans. with additions, M. B. Riddle, A Commentary on the Holy Scriptures: Critical, Doctrinal, and Homiletical, with Special Reference to Ministers and Students, ed. John Peter Lange, (series) translated and edited, Philip Schaff, New Testament, vol. 7 (Edinburgh: Clark, 1870; reprint, Grand Rapids: Zondervan, 1960), 72, 75, 77; John Eadie, *A Commentary on the Greek Text of the Epistle of Paul to the Ephesians*, ed. W. Young (Edinburgh: Clark, 1883; reprint, Grand Rapids: Baker, 1979), 130–31, 141; William Barclay, *The Letters to the Galatians and Ephesians*, rev. ed., Daily Study Bible (Philadelphia: Westminster, 1976), 95; Francis W. Beare and Theodore O. Wedel, "The Epistle to the Ephesians," in *Interpreter's Bible*, ed. George Arthur Buttrick, vol. 10 (New York: Abingdon, 1953), 638; J. N. Darby, *Synopsis of the Books of the Bible*, vol. 4, *Acts–Philippians* (New York: Loizeaux, n.d.; reprint, Oak Park, IL: Bible Truth, 1970), 397; E. K. Simpson, "Commentary on the Epistle to the Ephesians," in *Commentary on the Epistles to the Ephesians and Colossians* by E. K. Simpson and F. F. Bruce, New International Commentary on the New Testament, ed. Ned B. Stonehouse (Grand Rapids: Eerdmans, 1975), 46, 49, 51; John Gill, *Romans to Revelation*, Commentary on the Old and New Testaments, vol. 6 (London, Hill, 1854; reprint, Grand Rapids: Baker, 1980), 424; Archibald M. Hunter, *Galatians, Ephesians, Philippians, Colossians*, Layman's Bible Commentary, ed. Balmer H. Kelly, vol. 22 (Richmond, VA: Knox, 1959), 54–55; William MacDonald, *Believer's Bible Commentary: Old and New Testaments*, ed. Art Farstad (Nashville, TN: Nelson, 1995), 1916; R. Kent Hughes, *Ephesians: The Mystery of the Body of Christ*, Preaching the Word (Wheaton, IL: Crossway, 1990), 66; Ralph P. Martin, "Ephesians," in *2 Corinthians–Philemon*, Broadman Bible Commentary, ed. Clifton J. Allen, vol. 11 (Nashville, TN: Broadman, 1971), 140–41; F. F. Bruce, *The Epistles to the Colossians, to Philemon, and to the Ephesians*, New International Commentary on the New Testament, ed. F. F. Bruce (Grand Rapids: Eerdmans, 1984), 280, says, "'You' at the beginning of v. 1 probably means 'you Gentiles'. . . ." Cp. 283, 285.

Martin appears to agree, although his treatment is too terse to allow certainty.[19] The 1602 annotations to the Geneva Bible also support this position.[20] Hendricksen holds a similar view,[21] and is not disturbed by any apparent difficulties: "Now if this be a case of syntactical inconsistency it is one of the most glorious on record!"[22] Abbott holds this position as well,[23] and (*contra* Salmond and Alford) specifically seeks to refute the idea that πάντες (2:3) renders it impossible.

> The πάντες is certainly no objection to this. "Even amongst us (the chosen people) there was no exception." What more natural than to say "all of us also." If πάντες included both Jews and Gentiles, ἡμεῖς would be quite superfluous; and the emphatic καὶ ἡμεῖς would be unintelligible if it included ὑμεῖς of *vv*. 1 and 2.[24]

Charles Hodge also holds to this view, somewhat more enthusiastically than the others:

> It appears not only from ch. 1:11, 13, and from the connection to this place, but still more clearly from v. 11 and those following, in this chapter, that by *you* in this whole epistle, the apostle means Gentiles; and by *we*, when the pronouns are contrasted as here, the Jews.[25]

---

[19] Alfred Martin, "Ephesians," in *Wycliffe Bible Commentary*, ed. Charles F. Pfeiffer and Everett F. Harrison (Chicago: Moody Press, 1962), 1305–6.

[20] *The New Testament of our Lord Jesus Christ* (London: Barker, 1602); reprinted as *The Geneva Bible (The Annotated New Testament, 1602 edition)*, ed. Gerald T. Sheppard (New York: Pilgrim, 1989), 108.

[21] William Hendricksen, *Exposition of Ephesians*, New Testament Commentary (Grand Rapids: Baker, 1967), 109–10, 114–17.

[22] Hendricksen, *Ephesians*, 117.

[23] T. K. Abbott, *A Critical and Exegetical Commentary on the Epistles to the Ephesians and to the Colossians*, The International Critical Commentary on the Holy Scriptures of the Old and New Testaments, ed. Samuel Rolles Driver, Alfred Plummer, and Charles Augustus Briggs (Edinburgh: Clark, 1897), 43.

[24] Abbott, *Ephesians*, 43.

[25] Charles Hodge, *A Commentary on the Epistle to the Ephesians* (New York: Carter, 1856; reprint, Grand Rapids: Baker, 1982), 103.

Hodge fails to note that the parallel structure between *you being dead* and *us being dead* extends the contrast into 2:5a, and therefore sees *us* in 2:4 as a reference to all Christians.[26]

Position D

Position D has the distinction of holding the most restrictive[27] definition of both pronouns: *we* refers to Jewish believers and *you* to Gentile believers until they are united with Christ in vv. 5b–6. Because he catches the contrast Hodge missed, Robertson holds this view,[28] as does Niemelä.[29] There is ample evidence to support the point. Paul introduces the contrast between *you* and *we* in 1:11–14, where he speaks of *you* as latecomers to the gospel in which *we* had first believed. In isolation that passage might admit various interpretations, but the full context (e.g., 2:1–7, 11–12) brings the racial division to the forefront. Paul's further discussion of the union of Jewish and Gentile believer into *one new man*, with all that entails (2:13–22), and discourse on his ministry of proclaiming that mystery (3:1–13), only cement the racial nature of the contrast. One cannot possibly discuss the *union* of two disparate groups unless one first discusses *two disparate groups*—and having been thus defined as disparate, they will remain so until united. This is the purpose of the repeated contrast between *you* and *we*.

---

[26] Charles Hodge, *Ephesians*, 111.

[27] Position B would actually be more restrictive, but appears to be a null category.

[28] Archibald Thomas Robertson, *Word Pictures in the New Testament*, vol. 4, *The Epistles of Paul* (Nashville, TN: Broadman, 1931), 523–24.

[29] John H. Niemelä, "*If Anyone's Work Is Burned*: Scrutinizing Proof-Texts," *CTS Journal* 8 (January–March 2002): 29–31.

Position F

Position F maintains that Paul uses the pronouns interchangeably in this instance. Chafer's handling of the passage seems to presuppose this view. He initially appears to favor Position D or E, but his treatment is somewhat contradictory. On one hand, he clearly differentiates between *you* and *we* along racial lines: "The change from the use of 'you' to 'we' in these verses is significant, indicating, as it does, that this transforming blessing is for Jew and Gentile alike."[30] On the other hand, he asserts, "in verses 2 and 3, the present condition of all—both Jew and Gentile—who are out of Christ is disclosed."[31] One might understand that he was thinking of a respective treatment (i.e., Gentile in 2:2 and Jew in 2:3), but his subsequent treatment of "the estate of the lost"[32] in the passage does not distinguish the *you* statements from the *we* statements, handling them as though they all referred to every lost person.[33] MacArthur is also inconsistent. In his discussion of 2:1–3, he treats the pronouns in 2:1–3 as interchangeable, but then with reference to 2:5a, he says, "The **we** may emphasize the linking of the Jew with the Gentile 'you' in verse 1."[34] Max Turner's handling of the pronouns is equally ambiguous.[35] Kent, on the

---

[30] Lewis Sperry Chafer, *The Ephesian Letter Doctrinally Considered* (New York: Loizeaux, 1935), 64.

[31] Chafer, *Ephesian Letter*, 66.

[32] Chafer, *Ephesian Letter*, 66.

[33] Chafer, *Ephesian Letter*, 66–69, holds that Paul here makes four assertions about all of the lost: "They are dead in trespasses and sins," "They are walking according to the course of this world," They are walking according to the prince of the power of the air," and "They are by nature children of wrath."

[34] John F. MacArthur, Jr., *Ephesians*, MacArthur New Testament Commentary (Chicago: Moody Press, 1986), 52–57, 59.

[35] Max Turner, "Ephesians," in *New Bible Commentary*, 4th ed., edited by G. J. Wenham, J. A. Motyer, D. A. Carson, and R. T. France (Leicester and Downers Grove, IL: Inter-Varsity, 1994), 1228–29.

other hand, considers and explicitly rejects the idea that the pronouns refer to distinct groups:

> Many have felt that Paul was speaking of Gentile Christians in his reference to "you" (2:1) and then includes Jewish Christians in "also we all" (2:3). However, inasmuch as the verb which governs verse 1 is "made alive" in verse 5 . . . and the object found in verse 1—"you being dead in trespasses and sins"—is repeated in verse 5 as "we were dead in trespasses," it is doubtful whether Paul has such a sharp distinction in view.[36]

Others who make no distinction in this passage are Barlow, Martin, McGee, Mitton, Taylor, Lenksi, Pellegrin, Stott, Yeager, and Anders.[37]

Crucial Data

Any of the six positions except B (which makes no sense and enjoys little, if any, support) will provide sufficient basis for the theological argument of this thesis. The data point necessary for the argument is that all believers were formerly dead. Position F of course supports the point. Since positions A, C, and E all hold that *we* in 2:5 refers to all

---

[36] Homer A. Kent, Jr., *Ephesians: The Glory of the Church* (Chicago: Moody Press, 1971), 33. Kent fails to notice that the very features of the text he adduces are susceptible to interpretation as a small chiasm, which would support Position D (see page 29 for a brief description of the chiasm).

[37] George Barlow, *Galatians, Ephesians, Philippians, Colossians and I.–II. Thessalonians*, Preacher's Complete Homiletic Commentary, vol. 29 (New York: Funk & Wagnalls, n.d.), 148; Ralph P. Martin, "Ephesians," in *New Bible Commentary*, 3rd ed., edited by D. Guthrie and J. A. Motyer (Leicester: Inter-Varsity; Grand Rapids, Eerdmans, 1970), 1110; J. Vernon McGee, *Thru the Bible with J. Vernon McGee*, vol. 5 (Pasadena, CA: Thru the Bible Radio, 1983), 231–32; C. Leslie Mitton, *Ephesians*, New Century Bible Commentary, ed. Matthew Black. (London: Marshall, Morgan, and Scott, 1973; paperback reprint, London: Marshall, Morgan, and Scott; Grand Rapids: Eerdmans, 1981), 84; Willard H. Taylor, "Ephesians," in *Beacon Bible Commentary*, ed. A. F. Harper, et al., vol. 9 (Kansas City, MO: Beacon Hill, 1969), 170; R. C. H. Lenski, *The Interpretation of St. Paul's Epistles to the Galatians, to the Ephesians and to the Philippians* (Minneapolis, MN: Augsburg, 1937), 407; Harold F. Pellegrin, *The Epistle of Paul the Apostle to the Ephesians: Studies in the Christian Life* (Grand Rapids: Zondervan, 1937), 141, 149, 157–58; John R. W. Stott, *The Message of Ephesians: God's New Society*, The Bible Speaks Today, ed. John R. W. Stott (Leicester and Downers Grove, IL: Inter-Varsity, 1979), 71–79; Randolph O. Yeager, *The Renaissance New Testament*, vol. 14 (Gretna, LA: Pelican, 1983), 206, 210; Max Anders, *Galatians, Ephesians, Philippians & Colossians*, Holman New Testament Commentary, ed. Max Anders (Nashville, TN: Broadman & Holman, 1999), 110–11.

believers, they also support the necessary data point that all believers were once dead. The most restrictive view, Position D, also supports that data point since it sees *you* in 2:1 as a reference to Gentile believers and *we* in 2:5 as a reference to Jewish believers. Taken together, *you* and *we* include everyone.

MEANING OF *DEAD* AND *MADE ALIVE*

The second pair of issues in Ephesians 2:1–10 is the meaning of *dead* and *made alive*. Commentators universally regard them as essentially antithetical, such that whatever malady Paul has in mind as the meaning of *dead*, being *made alive* cures it. While most commentators and theologians agree on the essential nature of these terms, a minority view does exist.

The Essential Nature of the Terms

Moral/Experiential. While mentioning spiritual death in passing, Mitton seems to regard the focus of Paul's discussion as the experiential moral issues within man rather than man's standing relative to God:

> 'Death' is an apt description of the results of sin: constant repetition of evil does produce callousness (deadness) toward others whom the sin hurts and insensitivity towards the deterioration in one's own character which follows. . . . Life means a new awareness of what is meant by goodness and its claim upon us, a new sense of God's nearness to us and the peace which reconciliation with God brings, a sense that life has now begun to be something near what God meant it to be: authentic, abundant life.[38]

Barclay also focuses on the moral aspects of death.

> "Some have taken it to mean that without Christ men live in a state of sin which in the life to come produces the death of the soul. But Paul is not

---

[38] Mitton, *Ephesians*, 81–82.

talking about the life to come; he is talking about this present life. There are three directions in which the effect of sin is deadly.

> (i) Sin kills innocence. . . .
> (ii) Sin kills ideals. . . .
> (iii) In the end sin kills the will. . . . [39]

Barclay's treatment of *made alive* is consistent with this approach to death: he goes on to state how in making man alive, Jesus "take[s] away the sense of guilt which the lost innocence necessarily brings with it," "reawakens the ideal in the heart of man," and "revives and restores the lost will."[40] MacLaren appears to hold a similar view.[41]

Spiritual/Forensic. The majority view, however, holds that Paul has in mind the forensic, spiritual death which lies at the root of moral and experiential corruption.[42] Within that camp there are a variety of less significant differences. Most conceive of spiritual death as separation or alienation from God at the very least. As Calvin has it,

---

[39] Barclay, *Galatians and Ephesians*, 97–98.

[40] Barclay, *Galatians and Ephesians*, 102–3. While these assertions regarding the moral fruits of "death" may indeed be true, they miss the point of the figure in Ephesians: Paul is less concerned with these things than with their source: the state of "being alienated from the life of God" (Eph. 4:18).

[41] Alexander MacLaren, *Ephesians*, Expositions of Holy Scripture (London: Hodder and Stoughton, 1909; reprint, Grand Rapids: Baker, 1974), 82–85. Like Mitton he does mention spiritual death in passing (89, 99).

[42] Robertson, *Word Pictures*, vol. 4, 523; A. Skevington Wood, "Ephesians," in *NIV Bible Commentary*, ed. Kenneth L. Barker and John R. Kohlenberger, III, vol. 2, *New Testament* (Grand Rapids: Zondervan, 1994), 756; Alford, *Greek New Testament*, 88; Anders, *Ephesians*, 110; Salmond, "Ephesians," 283; Ralph P. Martin, "Ephesians," in *Broadman*, 141; Taylor, "Ephesians," 170; Chafer, *Ephesian Letter*, 67; Barth, *Ephesians*, 233; Abbott, *Ephesians*, 39; Charles Hodge, *Ephesians*, 96; Ernest Best, "Dead in Trespasses and Sins (Eph. 2.1)," in *Essays on Ephesians* (Edinburgh: Clark, 1997), 83–85; Turner, "Ephesians," 1229; Ralph P. Martin, "Ephesians," in *New Bible Commentary*, 1110; Alfred Martin, "Ephesians," 1305–6; MacDonald, *Believer's Bible Commentary*, 1916–17; Kent, *Ephesians*, 33, 36; Darby, *Synopsis*, vol. 4, 397–99; Gill, *Romans to Revelation*, 424, 426; Jamieson, Fausset, and Brown, *Commentary*, 1283–84; Braune, *Ephesians*, 78; Barlow, *Ephesians*, 148; Best, *Ephesians*, 215; Pellegrin, *Ephesians*, 141, 159; Hughes, *Ephesians*, 65–66; Stott, *Message of Ephesians*, 71; Bloomfield, *The Greek Testament*, vol. 2, 266–67; Yeager, *Renaissance New Testament*, vol. 14, 206, 215; Geerhardus Vos, "The Spiritual Resurrection of Believers: A Sermon on Ephesians 2:4,5," trans. Richard B. Gaffin, Jr., http://www.kerux.com/documents/ KeruxV5N1A1.asp (accessed July 21, 2003).

"As spiritual death is nothing else than the alienation of the soul from God, we are all born as dead men, and we live as dead men, until we are made partakers of the life of Christ. . . ."[43] Many others agree.[44] A few add that spiritual death involves alienation from resurrection life,[45] and the others would likely agree, since to be alienated from God is to be alienated from the resurrection life that He provides.

Paul's Emphasis. While Paul does comment on the moral effects of death, his focus lies elsewhere, as the framework of the passage itself demonstrates. The issue in the passage is not the moral effects of death or life, but the fact that believers were dead and were made alive in Christ. Paul does say certain things about death and life here (including the comments touching on the *ordo salutis* that are the focus of this thesis), but he does not offer definitions *per se*.

A brief look at the terms in other passages throughout the book adds a little light: the closely related use in 1:20 has Christ being raised *from among the dead ones*, the exhortation no longer to walk as the rest of the Gentiles in 4:17–19 characterizes them as *alienated from the life of God*, and the exhortation not to be fellow-inheritors of God's wrath with the *sons of disobedience* in 5:6–14 culminates in the hymnic command to badly-behaved (i.e., *sleeping*) believers to *arise from among the dead ones*. Thus,

---

[43] Calvin, *Galatians and Ephesians*, 219.

[44] Lenski, *St. Paul's Epistles*, 407; Anders, *Ephesians*, 119; Bruce, *Ephesians*, 280; Hoehner, "Ephesians," 622; *Ephesians,* 307–8; Beare and Wedel, "Ephesians," 638; McGee, *Thru the Bible*, 232; Barth, *Ephesians*, 233; Simpson, "Ephesians," 47; Ralph P. Martin, "Ephesians," in *New Bible Commentary*, 1110; Gill, *Romans to Revelation*, 424; Jamieson, Fausset, and Brown, *Commentary*, 1283; MacArthur, *Ephesians*, 52–53.

[45] E.g., Lincoln, *Ephesians*, 92; Barth, *Ephesians*, 233.

unbelievers are *dead*, i.e., *alienated from God's life*. Believers, having been united with Christ, who was raised *from among the dead ones*, have been *made alive together with Christ*, although some of them are *sleeping*—and this *among the dead ones*. If they continue napping in the spiritual morgue, they will become fellow-inheritors of God's (temporal) wrath together with the corpses who belong there.

In the rest of the book, the immoral activities of death are presented as something in which a believer can (but should not) still participate. So if Paul focuses in 2:1–10 on the fact of their former spiritual death and current possession of spiritual life, it seems unlikely that his focus is on activities (although 2:2–3 does mention them). Rather, he is addressing the underlying spiritual state which issues naturally in immoral acts in the unbeliever, and the spiritual life that makes such acts as unnatural as napping among the corpses in a morgue. Therefore, as the majority correctly concluded, death here is spiritual and forensic, a matter of alienation from God, the source of all life.

Death, Life, and Faith

In view of the object of this thesis, it is appropriate to examine the views of commentators and theologians on the subject of spiritual death as it relates to faith and spiritual life. In addition to alienation from God, the source of life, and the resurrection life He provides, some would also add that Paul's definition of spiritual death includes the notion of total inability to respond to God in any fashion whatever.[46]

---

[46] E.g., Hendricksen, *Ephesians*, 112; Eadie, *Ephesians*, 120–21; A. Skevington Wood, "Ephesians," in *Expositor's Bible Commentary*, edited by Frank E. Gaebelein, vol. 11, *Ephesians–Philemon* (Grand Rapids: Regency, 1978), 33; Vos, "Spiritual Resurrection."

Reformed Theology. Reformed theology argues that spiritual death is incompatible with faith in the gospel, or even with the desire to be saved:

> If man's nature is depraved, not simply in all of its parts, but in such a way that each part is thoroughly corrupt, then there is no good at all which man can perform in any sense of the word which is pleasing in the sight of God. He cannot do natural good. He cannot do spiritual good. He cannot do civil good. He cannot conform his nature to the law of God. *He cannot will his salvation.* He is bound hopelessly in the shackles of sin.[47]
>
> Because of the fall, man is unable of himself to savingly believe the gospel. The sinner is dead, blind and deaf to the things of God; his heart is deceitful and desperately corrupt. His will is not free, it is in bondage to his evil nature, therefore, he will not—indeed he cannot—choose good over evil in the spiritual realm. Consequently, it takes much more than the Spirit's assistance to bring a sinner to Christ—it takes regeneration by which the Spirit makes the sinner alive and gives him a new nature. Faith is not something man contributes to salvation but is itself a part of God's gift of salvation—it is God's gift to the sinner, not the sinner's gift to God.[48]

Thus regeneration must precede faith. Boettner says it well: "As a result of this change [regeneration] a man comes to see the truth and gladly accepts it."[49]

---

[47] Herman Hanko, "Total Depravity" in *The Five Points of Calvinism*, by Herman Hanko, Homer Hoeksema, and Gise J. Van Baren (Grand Rapids: Reformed Free, 1980), 20. Emphasis is added.

[48] David N. Steele and Curtis C. Thomas, *The Five Points of Calvinism: Defined, Defended, Documented*, International Library of Philosophy and Theology: Biblical and Theological Studies, ed. J. Marcellus Kik (Phillipsburg, NJ: Presbyterian & Reformed, 1963), 16.

[49] Loraine Boettner, *The Reformed Doctrine of Predestination*, 4th ed. (Grand Rapids: Eerdmans, 1936), 68, cp. "dead in trespasses and sins," 61. See also Wayne Grudem, *Systematic Theology: An Introduction to Bible Doctrine* (Grand Rapids: Zondervan, 1994), 701–2, which explicitly ties the idea to this passage; Arthur Pink, *The Doctrine of Salvation* (Grand Rapids: Baker, 1975), 30–31; Archibald Alexander Hodge, *Popular Lectures on Theological Themes* (Philadelphia, PA: Presbyterian Board, 1887), 143; Charles Hodge, *Systematic Theology*, vol. 2 (London and Edinburgh: Nelson; New York: Scribner, 1871), 260; E. C. Wines, *A Treatise on Regeneration* (Philadelphia, PA: Presbyterian Board, 1863), 15; Augustus Hopkins Strong, *Systematic Theology: A Compendium and Commonplace-Book Designed for the Use of Theological Students* (Philadelphia, PA: Judson, 1907), 793; R. C. Sproul, *Chosen By God* (Wheaton, IL: Tyndale House, 1986), 118; James Montgomery Boice, *Foundations of the Christian Faith: A Comprehensive & Readable Theology* (Downers Grove, IL: InterVarsity, 1986), 402–3; Louis Berkhof, *Systematic Theology*, 4th ed. (Grand Rapids: Eerdmans, 1941; reprint, Carlisle, PA: Banner of Truth Trust, 1958), 418; Thomas R. Schreiner and Ardel B. Caneday, *The Race Set Before Us: A Biblical Theology of Perseverance and Assurance* (Leicester and Downers Grove, IL: Inter-Varsity, 2001), 317.

This view lies at the very heart of Reformed theology. Calvin himself states this position in his commentary on John 1:13:

> Hence it follows, first, that faith does not proceed from ourselves, but is the fruit of spiritual regeneration; for the Evangelist affirms that no man can believe, unless he be begotten of God; and therefore faith is a heavenly gift. It follows, secondly, that faith is not bare or cold knowledge, since no man can believe who has not been renewed by the Spirit of God.[50]

Thus Reformed theology, from its very roots, has maintained that a spiritually dead man cannot desire salvation or exercise faith, but must first be regenerated in order that he be capable of desiring salvation and exercising faith.[51]

Arminian Theology. The Arminian view is not so different as one might suppose when it comes to the subject of death; it agrees with its Reformed roots on essentials. The difference lies in the purported means for escaping death. To the Reformer, as we have seen, saving faith is the result of regeneration, and so are repentance, conversion, and all else. Arguing against this view of the *ordo salutis*, Summers says,

> Strange that they do not see that before any one is made a child of God by regenerating grace, he has to use preventing grace so as to repent, believe and call upon God. . . .
> As we have seen, a man will continue in choosing and doing evil, unless by divine influence he is shown what is good and urged to choose it. Now preventing grace is that influence. It precedes our action, and gives us the capacity to will and to do right, enlightening the intellect, and exciting the sensibility. . . . All this is brought to bear upon the sinner [in

---

[50] John Calvin, *Commentary on the Gospel According to John*, vol. 1, trans. William Pringle (Edinburgh: Calvin Translation Society, n.d.; reprint, Grand Rapids: Baker, 1981), 43–44.

[51] Examining the internal coherence of this theology is beyond the scope of this thesis (which examines its correspondence with the text of Ephesians 2:1–10). Roy L. Aldrich, "The Gift of God," *Bibliotheca Sacra* 122 (July–September 1965): 248–53, does discuss the subject, and offers a telling challenge to certain elements within Calvinism.

order] that he can be the subject of "faith and calling upon God," if he chooses; or, if he chooses, he can decline to do so, and "do despite to the Spirit of grace." Mr. Wesley, in his sermon on "Working out Our Own Salvation," says:

> For, allowing that all the souls of men are dead in sin by *nature*, this excuses none, seeing there is no man that is in a state of mere nature; there is no man, unless he has quenched the Spirit, that is wholly void of the grace of God.[52]

A careful reader will note that far from disputing the Reformed conception of spiritual death, Summers concedes it, but then stipulates that God's universally available "preventing grace" supernaturally enables a spiritually dead man to exercise faith toward God *despite his deadened state, which would not allow it*. The approving quote from Wesley only confirms this. Earlier in the referenced sermon, Wesley says,

> Seeing all men are by nature not only sick, but "dead in trespasses and sins," it is not possible for them to do anything well till God raises them from the dead. It was impossible for Lazarus to come forth, till the Lord had given him life. And it is equally impossible for us to *come* out of our sins, yea, or to make the least motion toward it, till He who hath all power in heaven and earth calls our dead souls into life.[53]

One must ask at this point whether Wesley sees faith as doing something well, as a "motion toward" coming out of sins. The same sermon indicates that he does, because he understands it as the culmination of prevenient grace:

> Salvation begins with what is usually termed (and very properly) *preventing grace*; including the first wish to please God, the first dawn of light concerning his will, and the first slight transient conviction of having sinned against him. All these imply some tendency toward life; some degree of salvation; the beginning of a deliverance from a blind, unfeeling heart, quite insensible of God and the things of God. Salvation is carried

---

[52] Thos. O. [Thomas Osmond] Summers, *Systematic Theology: A Complete Body of Wesleyan Arminian Divinity*, edited, revised, and annotated by Jno. J. [John James] Tigert (Nashville, TN: Methodist Episcopal Church, South, 1888), 76.

[53] Wesley, John. "On Working out our own Salvation," in *Sermons on Several Occasions: Second Series* (N.p.: n.p., 1788); reprinted in *The Works of John Wesley*, 3rd ed., vol. 6, (London: Wesleyan Methodist Book Room, 1872; reprint, Grand Rapids: Baker, 1979), 511–12.

on by *convincing grace*, usually in Scripture termed *repentance;* which brings a larger measure of self-knowledge, and a farther deliverance from the heart of stone. Afterwards we experience the proper Christian salvation; whereby, through grace, we "are saved by faith;" consisting of those two grand branches, justification and sanctification.[54]

Article VIII of Wesley's "Methodist Articles of Religion" states substantially the same position.

> The condition of man after the fall of Adam is such that he can not turn and prepare himself, by his own natural strength and works, to faith and calling upon God; wherefore we have no power to do good works, pleasant and acceptable to God, without the grace of God by Christ preventing us, that we may have a good will, and working with us, when we have that good will.[55]

In this respect Wesley is thoroughly in accord with Arminius himself:

> Evangelical and saving faith is of such vast excellency as to exceed the entire nature of man, and all his understanding, even that of Adam when placed in a state of innocence. . . . [56]

Arminius then makes the bald claim "Faith is a gracious and gratuitous gift of God. . . ."[57] Arminian theology, from its very roots, has maintained that spiritual death by its nature precludes man from any exercise of faith in the gospel, such that God must graciously grant him the faith in order that he be capable of believing.

---

[54] Wesley, "Working," 509.

[55] Philip Schaff, ed., *The Creeds of Christendom*, 6th ed., rev. David S. Schaff, vol. 3, *The Evangelical Protestant Creeds* (New York: Harper & Row, 1931; reprint, Grand Rapids: Baker, 1998), 809.

[56] James Arminius, "Certain Articles to be Diligently Examined and Weighed," in *The Works of James Arminius*, trans. James Nichols, vol. 2 (London: Longman, Rees, Orme, Brown, and Green, 1828; reprint, Grand Rapids: Baker, 1999), 723.

[57] Arminius, "Certain Articles," 723.

Common Ground Between Reformed and Arminian Theologies. Arminians differ from their Calvinistic roots with respect to prevenient grace and the *ordo salutis* (by placing faith before regeneration). However, they also demonstrate some important continuities with the Reformed tradition. By injecting the concept of prevenient grace, the Arminians have been able to maintain their *ordo salutis* while also accepting a Reformed view of faith and spiritual death. Baker describes the commonality between the Reformed and Arminian views in this way:

> Most theologians, including both Calvinists and Arminians, agree that the Fall left man in a depraved condition. The Arminian supposes that God extends to all men such a measure of common grace as to enable all to exercise faith in God if they will. The Calvinist supposes that God extends irresistible grace to the elect which guarantees that they will exercise saving faith and that He passes by the non-elect. Faith, therefore, is the gift of God and not the product of man's nature. Such passages as Ephesians 2:8 and Philippians 1:29 are used as proof texts. The general impression is given that faith is a kind of good works and that if the natural man exercised faith of his own accord it would mean that man was partly saved by his own good works.[58]

Thus, the common ground between Calvinism and its Arminian offshoot lies in their common understanding of the fundamental incompatibility of saving faith (a positive movement toward God, with which God may be pleased) and spiritual death (a state which precludes any such movement). The Reformed theologian faces the implications, placing regeneration before faith in his *ordo salutis*. The Arminian interjects the miracle of prevenient grace to explain how faith can occur in the spiritually dead.

---

[58] Charles F. Baker, *A Dispensational Theology*, 2nd ed. (Grand Rapids: Grace Bible College Publications, 1971), 420–21. Note that R. C. Sproul, *Chosen By God* (Wheaton, IL: Tyndale House, 1986), 118, explicitly affirms this conception of faith: "Faith is not monergistic."

Crucial Data

The meaning of *dead*, then, is forensic spiritual death, of which all believers were formerly willing victims. At very least, such a state constitutes alienation from God, the source of spiritual life. *Made alive* refers to the miracle of regeneration, in which God removes a sinner from his alienated state and brings him into communion with Himself. Significant portions of the interpretive tradition, notably both the Reformed and Arminian branches of theology, carry the meaning of *dead* further, seeing it as antithetical to faith. For the Reformed, this antithesis prohibits the dead exercising saving faith under any circumstances, while for the Arminian, the antithesis requires the initial action of prevenient grace to mitigate the effects of spiritual death.

RELATION OF *BY GRACE YOU ARE SAVED* TO ITS CONTEXTS
By Grace You Are Saved *in 2:5*

The third paired issue under consideration in the passage is the relationship of *by grace you are saved* to its context both places the expression occurs (2:5 and 2:8). The vast majority of the commentators refer to the first occurrence (2:5) as parenthetical, although some do not state the nature of the parenthetical relationship.[59] Eadie refers to the parenthesis as an interjection or digression,[60] but most commentators see the three main verbs of the sentence ("made alive together," "raised up together," and "seated

---

[59] Robertson, *Word Pictures*, vol. 4, 524; Anders, *Ephesians*, 112; Bruce, *Ephesians*, 286; Beare and Wedel, "Ephesians," 644; Turner, "Ephesians," 85; Hunter, *Ephesians*, 56; Alfred Martin, "Ephesians," 1306.

[60] Eadie, *Ephesians*, 145, 149.

together") as equated with, or a subset of, by-grace salvation.[61] Alford sees them as "a notable example" of by-grace salvation,[62] while Lenski goes further, stating that *by grace you are saved* is "the thought that underlies this entire paragraph."[63]

But is the majority correct? Does *by grace you are saved* relate to the main verbs of the sentence? Consider the alternatives. Begin with the concept that Paul's argument either makes sense or it does not (i.e., makes nonsense). Any orthodox interpreter must presuppose that Paul (and the Holy Spirit) will not make nonsense in a passage, not even in a single clause. On that basis, one must conclude that every word, every clause, has a communicative purpose. Furthermore, the purpose of a clause cannot be knowable if it cannot be discerned on the basis of its context.[64]

---

[61] Lincoln, *Ephesians*, 102; Mitton, *Ephesians*, 90–91; Hendricksen, *Ephesians*, 117; Lenski, *St. Paul's Epistles*, 417; Salmond, "Ephesians," 288; Wood, "Ephesians," in *Expositor's*, 35; Taylor, "Ephesians," 173; Hoehner, "Ephesians," 623; *Ephesians*, 331; McGee, *Thru the Bible*, vol. 5, 235; Perkins, "Ephesians," 392; Barth, *Ephesians*, 220–21; Simpson, "Ephesians," 52; Abbott, *Ephesians*, 49; Charles Hodge, *Ephesians*, 113; Kent, *Ephesians*, 37; Gill, *Romans to Revelation*, 426; Jamieson, Fausset, and Brown, *Commentary*, 1248; Braune, *Ephesians*, 78; MacLaren, *Expositions*, vol. 13, 99 (although he is somewhat unclear); Stott, *Message of Ephesians*, 80–81; Yeager, *Renaissance New Testament*, vol. 14, 215; Best, *Ephesians*, 216–17; Niemelä, "*Anyone's Work*," 28–29.

[62] Alford, *Greek New Testament*, 94.

[63] Lenski, *St. Paul's Epistles*, 421–22.

[64] The meaning is either private and multivalent, centered on the reader's experience of the text, or it is publicly accessible and unified. No orthodox interpreter can consistently maintain the former (especially in passages like Luke 1:4; 1 Timothy 3:15; and 1 John 5:13.) If the latter, the clues to meaning, the criteria by which one can discern that an utterance means A and not B, must also be public. And if the author intends for readers to understand the text, then he will place the clues to meaning in plain sight, not under a rock someplace, hence the primacy of context, the more immediate the better. For further discussion on context providing public criteria for interpretation, see E. D. Hirsch, Jr., *Validity in Interpretation* (New Haven, CT: Yale University Press, 1967); E. D. Hirsch, Jr., *The Aims of Interpretation* (Chicago: University of Chicago Press, 1976); Elliott E. Johnson, *Expository Hermeneutics: An Introduction* (Grand Rapids: Academie, 1990); Umberto Eco, *The Limits of Interpretation* (Indianapolis: Indiana University Press, 1990); Umberto Eco, et al., *Interpretation and Overinterpretation*, ed. Stefan Collini (New York: Cambridge University Press, 1992).

If *by grace you are saved* is a digression without any relation to the context (and with no indication that he intends such a digression), then how is a reader to understand the meaning? A completely unrelated thought would obscure the true meaning of his text as readers warped both the digression and its context out of shape to make them fit together.[65] If it does relate to its context, then one must ask, to what does it relate? Only one answer satisfies the requirements of the context: to the main clause of 2:1–7. Three contextual signals closely relate the three main verbs to each other: their shared subject, καὶ . . . καὶ, and the συν- prefixes. Paul could hardly have interjected *by grace you are saved* into the midst of those verbs unless he expected his readers to relate the parenthetical clause to the main verbs.

In what way does the parenthesis relate to the main clause? According to the main clause, believers were formerly *dead*. How does one *save* a *dead* man? By *making him alive*. And did these now-living men deserve this miracle? No indeed. They were not merely *dead*; they were *dead in sins*, therefore their salvation was accomplished *by grace*. When Paul writes *by grace you are saved*, he might have a great deal more in mind beyond being *made alive together with Christ*. From the context, he might also have in mind being *raised together and seated together in the heavenly places in Christ Jesus*, and perhaps a great deal more besides. But there can be no doubt that *made alive* is part of being *saved by grace*.

---

[65] The author's intent to communicate propositional content entitles the reader to presuppose that the utterance is coherent. Some types of literature do not intend to communicate propositional content, or do not intend to communicate at all (e.g., certain forms of modern poetry). In those genres, different rules of interpretation obtain, but in the literary work at hand, communication is indeed the goal.

By Grace You Are Saved *in 2:8*

Paul repeats the clause in 2:8, with the addition of τῇ γὰρ. Some commentators understand the article as anaphoric,[66] but the repetition in this context of the exact wording χάριτί ἐστε σεσῳσμένοι would be anaphoric even without the article. Another explanation for the article's presence is more likely, as the next paragraph will demonstrate. The γὰρ naturally relates 2:8–9 to the preceding sentence. As Lenski understands it, "So important is 'grace' that he not only repeats the parenthetical statement but now amplifies it as an explanation of (γὰρ) all that he says."[67] While others stop short of having "grace" as "an explanation of all that he says" in the passage, the majority regard *by grace you are saved* as resuming the thought of the same words in 2:5.

The majority is correct: the passage demands a link between 2:5 and 2:8. The reader sees Paul summarize his main thought in 2:1–7 in those potent three words χάριτί ἐστε σεσῳσμένοι (*by grace you are saved*), and now comes upon the same clause at the beginning of the next sentence. No coherent reader would suppose Paul to be taking up a new topic in the same words.[68] In this context, the expression requires no article to make

---

[66] E.g., Salmond, "Ephesians," 289; Best, *Ephesians*, 225; F. Blass and A. Debrunner, *A Greek Grammar of the New Testament and other Early Christian Literature*, trans. and rev., Robert W. Funk (Chicago: University of Chicago Press, 1961), 134–35.

[67] Lenski, *St. Paul's Epistles*, 422.

[68] Lincoln, *Ephesians*, 111; Robertson, *Word Pictures*, vol. 4, 525; Wood, "Ephesians," in *Expositor's*, 34–35; "Ephesians," in *NIV Bible Commentary*, 758; Mitton, *Ephesians*, 93; Alford, *Greek New Testament*, 94; Eadie, *Ephesians*, 149; Anders, *Ephesians*, 112; Bruce, *Ephesians*, 289; Salmond, "Ephesians," 289; Taylor, "Ephesians," 173; Hoehner, "Ephesians," 624; *Ephesians*, 340; Beare and Wedel, "Ephesians," 644; Barth, *Ephesians*, 221, 224; Abbott, *Ephesians*, 51; Charles Hodge, *Ephesians*, 117–18; Hunter, *Ephesians*, 56; Alfred Martin, "Ephesians," 1306; Gill, *Romans to Revelation*, 426; Jamieson, Fausset, and Brown, *Commentary*, 1248; Braune, *Ephesians*, 80; MacLaren, *Expositions*, vol. 13, 99 (perhaps); Best, *Ephesians*, 225.

it anaphoric—it could hardly be otherwise. Why then the article? If Paul wished to preserve the integrity of that key clause in order to heighten the effect of his repetition, and wished also to use γὰρ to connect 2:8–9 with 2:1–7, the article was necessary. Otherwise, the postpositive γὰρ would have required χάριτί γὰρ ἐστε σεσῳσμένοι.

RELATION OF *THROUGH FAITH* TO ITS CONTEXT

The final textual issue to examine in the interpretive tradition is the relationship of *through faith* to its context. The commentators use a varied terminology to refer to this relationship, but there is a common theme. Calvin furnishes a suitable introduction.

> On one side, we must look at God; and, on the other, at man. God declares, that he owes us nothing; so that salvation is not a reward or recompense, but unmixed grace. The next question is, in what way do men receive that salvation which is offered to them by the hand of God? The answer is, *by faith;* and hence he concludes that nothing connected with it is our own. If, on the part of God, it is grace alone, and if we bring nothing but faith, which strips us of all commendation, it follows that salvation does not come from us.[69]

While differing substantially on the definition of πίστις itself,[70] Barth agrees with Calvin with respect to the relationship between faith and salvation.[71] Countess concurs: ". . . the Apostle regards FAITH as the *medium* through which salvation is personally

---

[69] Calvin, *Galatians and Ephesians*, 227.

[70] Barth, *Ephesians*, 224–25, improperly considers πίστις (*faith*) to involve three things simultaneously: God's faithfulness, man's faithfulness, and man's faith. Eph. 2:9 shows that πίστις (*faith*) cannot involve man's faithfulness: οὐκ ἐξ ἔργων, ἵνα μή τις καυχήσηται (*not of works, lest anyone should boast*). By-grace salvation cannot be through faith *and* not of works, if man's faithfulness were bound up in the very concept of faith. While undoubtedly God's faithfulness is required, that is not what Paul's theology has in view for πίστις (*faith*). Note how in the preceding context (1:13–15) Paul equates πίστις (*faith*) with the Ephesians' belief in *the gospel of* [their] *salvation*. Nor is that identification unusual for Paul; see also Rom. 4:5, 11; 2 Cor. 4:13; Gal. 2:16. Obviously God must be trustworthy for man's faith to avail anything, but that does not make God's trustworthiness a part of the semantic range of πίστις (*faith*) in this context.

[71] Barth, *Ephesians*, 224.

appropriated and not that faith is the *cause* or *basis* of this salvation,"[72] and others state the issue in similar terms.[73] The 1602 Annotated New Testament edition of the Geneva Bible contains the following description of 2:4ff:

> Now hereof followeth another member of the comparison, declaring our excelencie, to wit, that by the vertue of Christ we are deliuered from that death, and made partakers of eternall life, to the ende that at length wee may reigne with him. And by diuers and sundry meanes hee beateth this into their heads, that the efficient cause of this benefit is the free mercie of God: and Christ himselfe is the materiall cause: and faith is the instrument. . . .[74]

Salmond states the relationship thus: ". . . by faith as the instrument or means. Paul never says διὰ τὴν πίστιν, as if the faith were the ground or procuring cause of the salvation. It is the χάριτι, too, not the explanatory πίστεως that has the first place in Paul's thoughts here."[75] A number of others also use the term *instrument*.[76] The distinction between the roles of grace and faith in salvation can appropriately be described in terms of principal cause *versus* instrumental cause.

> A "principal" cause is an efficient cause which produces an effect **in virtue of its own power.** An "instrumental" cause is an efficient cause which produces an effect **in virtue of the power of another cause.** Principal and instrumental causes are correlatives; the one implies the other.

---

[72] Robert H. Countess, "Thank God for the Genitive," *Journal of the Evangelical Theological Society* 12 (Spring 1969): 118.

[73] Ralph P. Martin, "Ephesians," in *New Bible Commentary*, 1110; Alfred Martin, "Ephesians," 1306; Kent, *Ephesians*, 38; Best, *Ephesians*, 226.

[74] *The Geneva Bible*, 108. Spelling is preserved from the original, but replacing the old medial *s* with the modern form.

[75] Salmond, "Ephesians," 289.

[76] Gill, *Romans to Revelation*, 427; Jamieson, Fausset, and Brown, *Commentary*, 1284; Braune, *Ephesians*, 80; Barlow, *Ephesians*, 154; MacLaren, *Expositions*, vol. 13, 106.

> A carpenter uses a saw to cut a board; the saw is the instrumental cause, the carpenter is the principal cause. A hunter kills a deer by shooting it with his rifle; the rifle is the instrumental cause performing its action under the direction and control of the hunter.
> It should be noted that both causes exert their own peculiar causality. The saw cuts and the rifle shoots; but they would not act at all and not in this particular manner, were it not for the direction and control of the principal cause.[77]

In their own chosen terminology, what each commentator affirms is this: faith is the *instrumental* cause of salvation, but grace is the *principal* cause.[78]

CONCLUSION

This chapter has reviewed the commentary literature at seven key points. The reader who has been following along on the grammatical diagrams on pages 17–18 will notice that all of these key points occur in the emphasized text (i.e., the core propositions and their nonverbal modifiers or the concessive clauses) as discussed in Chapter 2. Before proceeding, it will be helpful to look back at these points, since they are the factual foundation upon which the theological reasoning of the next chapter will rest.

The Identity of You *and* We

Five basic positions are available in the commentary literature. All five positions lead to the conclusion that Paul says *all* believers were once *dead*, and have been *made alive*. Position F obviously would support this conclusion since it recognizes no

---

[77] "Efficient Causality: The Traditional View of Classical Realism" http://radicalacademy.com/studentrefphil6j.htm (accessed Feb. 20, 2004).

[78] Lincoln, *Ephesians*, 111; Wood, "Ephesians," in *Expositor's*, 36; "Ephesians," in *NIV Bible Commentary*, 758; Alford, *Greek New Testament*, 94; Lenski, *St. Paul's Epistles*, 422; Eadie, *Ephesians*, 149–50; Anders, *Ephesians*, 112; Bruce, *Ephesians*, 289; Ralph P. Martin, "Ephesians," in *Broadman*, 143; Hoehner, "Ephesians," 624; *Ephesians*, 341; Beare and Wedel, "Ephesians," 644; Simpson, "Ephesians," 54–55; Abbott, *Ephesians*, 51; Charles Hodge, *Ephesians*, 118; Robertson, *Word Pictures*, vol. 4, 582.

distinction between first and second person pronouns in this passage.[79] Positions A, C and E also support the conclusion, since they define *we* in 2:4–7 as explicit references to all believers.[80] Position D—that *you* refers to Gentile believers exclusively and *we* refers to Jewish believers exclusively, until the two are united with Christ in 2:5b–6—has the most restrictive definitions. But it still leads to the same conclusion: all believers (both Jew and Gentile) were once *dead* and have been *made alive*.

The Meaning of Dead *and* Made Alive

The two expressions are obviously paired: the very nature of the figure demands that the latter cures the former. Except for a few aberrations, the commentators correctly understand *dead* to refer to forensic spiritual death, which at the very least means alienation from God, the sole source of spiritual life. *Made alive* therefore refers to regeneration, i.e., God raising the spiritually dead to spiritual life.[81]

The Relation of By Grace You Are Saved *to its Contexts*

The first *by grace you are saved*, the parenthetical comment in 2:5, summarizes (or alternately, includes) the three main verbs of the sentence: *made alive together*, *raised up together*, and *seated together*. *By grace* indicates the undeserved nature of this action, and corresponds to the discussion in 2:1–4, 7. The reuse of the clause (in 2:8) resumes the same thought, taking the germ of the concept from 2:5 and expanding on it in 2:8–9.[82]

---

[79] See discussion on pages 50–51.

[80] See discussion on pages 42–49.

[81] See discussion on pages 52–61.

[82] See discussion on pages 61–65.

The Relation of **Through Faith** *to its Context*

The principal cause of salvation is grace: grace, through its own virtue, is capable of saving dead sinners. However, the instrumental cause, the "trigger" that differentiates between the saved and the lost, is faith. Salvation occurs by means of grace, through the instrumentality of faith.[83]

---

[83] See discussion on pages 65–67.

CHAPTER 5

CONNECTING THE DOTS:

THE *ORDO SALUTIS* IN EPHESIANS 2:1–10

INTRODUCTION

The argument of this chapter takes the form of six syllogisms based on the points of textual data discussed in the preceding chapter. Each term will be numbered by syllogism and by term within the syllogism. For example, the middle term of the third syllogism will be 3–2. Following each syllogism, brief discussion of the evidence for each term will appear.[1]

THE ARGUMENT

Syllogism One

    1–1   All believers were once *dead*

    1–2   *Dead* refers to spiritual death.

    1–3   Therefore, all believers were once spiritually dead.

Little real controversy surrounds the first syllogism. The five principal positions on the meaning of the pronouns *you* and *we* end up affirming 1–1, despite their differences. With a few ill-conceived exceptions, the interpretive tradition affirms 1–2 as well; in fact, many directly draw the inference, 1–3.[2]

---

[1] This format is uncommon in theological literature, but Douglas R. Hofstadter's Pulitzer-winning *Gödel, Escher, Bach: An Eternal Golden Braid* (New York: Basic, 1979) used it frequently. Many of Alvin Plantinga's works use it as well, e.g., *Does God Have a Nature?* Aquinas Lecture 44 (Milwaukee: Marquette University Press, 1980); *God and Other Minds: A Study of the Rational Justification of Belief in God* (London and Ithaca, NY: Cornell University Press, 1967); and *God, Freedom and Evil* (New York: Harper and Row, 1974; reprint, Grand Rapids: Eerdmans, 1978).

[2] For evidence behind 1–1, see pages 41–52; for 1–2, see pages 52–55; for 1–3, see pages 52–55.

Syllogism Two

2–1   All believers were *made alive*.

2–2   *Made alive* refers to spiritual life (regeneration).

2–3   Therefore, all believers received spiritual life (regeneration).

The lack of controversy surrounding the first syllogism extends to the second. Whatever their interpretation of *dead* and *made alive*, commentators uniformly view the latter as the cure for the former.[3] Thus, if all believers once suffered from being *dead*, they have now been *made alive*. As with 1–2, so also with 2–2: only a few commentators would disagree, and those for poor reasons.[4] Again, many commentators explicitly draw the inference, 2–3.[5]

Syllogism Three

3–1   *By grace you are saved* (2:5) is parenthetical to *made alive* (and *raised up* and *seated*).

3–2   The parenthetical relation indicates that *made alive* (and *raised up* and *seated*) is equated with, or a subset of, *by grace you are saved*.

3–3   Therefore, *made alive* (and *raised up* and *seated*) is equated with, or a subset of, *saved* (2:5).

3–1 is grammatically necessary. No other explanation accounts for the presence of the second-person χάριτί ἐστε σεσῳσμένοι (*by grace you are saved*) in the middle of the main clause of the sentence.[6] The interpretive tradition is virtually unanimous in its

---

[3] See pages 52–55.

[4] See pages 52–55.

[5] See pages 52–60.

[6] See pages 61–63.

agreement with 3–2 on the relation indicated by the parenthesis, and the passage allows no other understanding in any case.[7] The commentators sometimes explicitly draw the implication, 3–3.[8]

Syllogism Four

    4–1   *Made alive* (and *raised up* and *seated*) is equated with, or a subset of, *saved* (2:5).

    4–2   *By grace you are saved* (2:8) resumes the topic of discussion from 2:5.

    4–3   Therefore, *made alive* (and *raised up* and *seated*) is equated with, or a subset of, *by grace you are saved* (2:8).

4–1 is the previously demonstrated conclusion of the third syllogism (3–3). 4–2 explicitly links χάριτί ἐστε σεσῳσμένοι (*by grace you are saved*) in 2:8 with the same expression in 2:5. Again, the interpretive tradition is close to unanimous in its support of that proposition, and the text itself provides strong support.[9] 4–3 is the necessary inference, but the interpretive tradition rarely if ever attests it.

Syllogism Five

    5–1   *Through faith* indicates the instrumental cause of *by grace you are saved* (2:8).

    5–2   *Made alive* (and *raised up* and *seated*) is equated with, or a subset of, *by grace you are saved* (2:8).

    5–3   Therefore, *through faith* is the instrumental cause of *made alive* (and *raised up* and *seated*).

---

[7] See pages 61–63.

[8] See pages 61–63.

[9] See pages 64–65.

Although the language used to describe the relationship varies considerably, the interpretive tradition almost unanimously supports 5–1.[10] 5–2 was previously established as 4–3. The inference, 5–3, does not appear to be drawn in the interpretive tradition.

Syllogism Six

      6–1   *Through faith* is the instrumental cause of *made alive* (and *raised up* and *seated*).

      6–2   Instrumental cause necessarily precedes its effect.

      6–3   Therefore, faith precedes being made alive (regeneration).

And here lies the rub for the Reformed *ordo salutis*. 6–1 was established previously as 5–3. Argument with 6–2 is not possible outside the realm of science fiction: time travel is the only conceivable means by which an effect can precede its cause.[11] The necessary inference, 6–3, is that faith precedes the reception of spiritual life.

---

[10] See pages 65–67.

[11] Actually, opinions vary from author to author as to whether causality paradoxes are possible even in time travel.

CONCLUSION

Assembled together, the full argument looks like this:

1–1 All believers were once *dead*
1–2 *Dead* refers to spiritual death.
1–3 Therefore, all believers were once spiritually dead.

2–1 All believers were *made alive*.
2–2 *Made alive* refers to spiritual life (regeneration).
2–3 Therefore, all believers received spiritual life (regeneration).

3–1 *By grace you are saved* (2:5) is parenthetical to *made alive* (and *raised up* and *seated*).
3–2 The parenthetical relation indicates that *made alive* (and *raised up* and *seated*) is equated with, or a subset of, *by grace you are saved*.
3–3 Therefore, *made alive* (and *raised up* and *seated*) is equated with, or a subset of, *saved* (2:5).

4–1 *Made alive* (and *raised up* and *seated*) is equated with, or a subset of, *saved* (2:5).
4–2 *By grace you are saved* (2:8) resumes the topic of discussion from 2:5.
4–3 Therefore, *made alive* (and *raised up* and *seated*) is equated with, or a subset of, *by grace you are saved* (2:8).

5–1 *Through faith* indicates the instrumental cause of *by grace you are saved* (2:8).
5–2 *Made alive* (and *raised up* and *seated*) is equated with, or a subset of, *by grace you are saved* (2:8).
5–3 Therefore, *through faith* is the instrumental cause of *made alive* (and *raised up* and *seated*).

6–1 *Through faith* is the instrumental cause of *made alive* (and *raised up* and *seated*).
6–2 Instrumental cause necessarily precedes its effect.
6–3 Therefore, faith precedes being made alive (regeneration).

If the text itself claims (as it does) that faith precedes regeneration, then an exegete must conclude that the nature of spiritual death is other than many suppose. Spiritually dead men do believe—must believe—for only in so doing can they be made spiritually alive: *quod erat demonstratum*. For interpreters approaching the Scriptures from a Reformed position, this conclusion is most unwelcome. Sadly, their theology has allowed them to eisegete inability to believe into *dead*. That eisegesis blinds them to the implications of the passage, because it introduces a definition not merely foreign to the passage, but directly in contradiction to it—and this while *agreeing with the data at issue*, as Chapter 4 demonstrates.[12]

The Arminian theologian should not feel that he has escaped unscathed: his view of spiritual death is such that he must import into the passage a prevenient grace which enables an *otherwise unable* dead man to believe. While the passage does not directly refute this view, neither does it require or even allude to it.[13] For Paul, the idea that dead men believe does not require additional explanation here.

---

[12] See pages 41–69.

[13] Χάρις (*grace*) in the two occurrences of χάριτί ἐστε σεσῳσμένοι (*by grace you are saved*) cannot refer to prevenient grace. On the Arminian scheme, the grace that saves goes well beyond the prevenient grace given to everyone. Man receives saving grace only *after* his proper response to prevenient grace culminates in faith in the gospel.

CHAPTER 6

THE ANTECEDENT OF ΤΟΥΤΟ

INTRODUCTION

"Very well," someone might say, "faith precedes regeneration. But manifestly faith cannot come from man: he is dead, insensible, unable to respond to God. Whence faith, then? Clearly from God, who by His miraculous grace grants to man the gift of faith in order that He might then regenerate him." Many hold just such a view of faith's origins, albeit without any accommodation to the *ordo salutis* demonstrated in Chapter 5. Those who hold that faith is a gift from God frequently claim support from Ephesians 2:8. The theological contention *faith is a gift of God* is not coextensive with the grammatical contention *πίστεως is the antecedent of τοῦτο*. The latter would prove the former, but the theological point does not depend only on that grammatical line of evidence. Any understanding of the grammar here admits the *possibility* that faith is a divine gift; at issue is whether the grammar here proves—or even addresses—it.[1]

Since the theological significance of the antecedent of τοῦτο directly bears on the interpretation of the framework of the passage at hand, and since it also directly bears on the theological argument of this thesis, this chapter will take up the issue. Wallace's *Greek Grammar Beyond the Basics* provides an outstanding summary of extant views. Accordingly, this chapter will begin by examining the four views Wallace adduces, and will then proceed to an analysis of the text itself to reach a conclusion.

---

[1] As with many other arguments, the question here is not whether the passage lends its support to one side of the argument or the other, but whether it lends support to *either* side.

AN ANALYSIS OF WALLACE

Wallace's willingness to list exegetically significant (and therefore controversial) examples of grammatical categories is one of the great strengths of his *Greek Grammar Beyond the Basics*. In the course of his discussion of demonstrative pronouns, Wallace gives an extended (for a grammar) discussion of four possible views of the antecedent of τοῦτο in Ephesians 2:8:

> The standard interpretations include: (1) "grace" as antecedent, (2) "faith" as antecedent, (3) the concept of a grace-by-faith salvation as antecedent, and (4) καὶ τοῦτο having an adverbial force with no antecedent ("and especially").
>
> The first and second options suffer from the fact that τοῦτο is neuter while χάριτι and πίστεως are feminine. Some have argued that the gender shift causes no problem because (a) there are other examples in Greek literature in which a neuter demonstrative refers back to a noun of a different gender, and (b) the τοῦτο has been attracted to the gender of δῶρον, the predicate nominative. These two arguments need to be examined together.
>
> While it is true that on rare occasions there is a gender shift between antecedent and pronoun, the pronoun is almost always caught between two nouns of different gender. One is the antecedent; the other is the predicate nom. . . . The construction in Eph 2:8, however, is not parallel because δῶρον is not the predicate nom. of τοῦτο, but of the implied "it" in the following clause. On a grammatical level, then, it is doubtful that either "faith" or "grace" is the antecedent of τοῦτο.
>
> More plausible is the third view, viz., that τοῦτο refers to the concept of a grace-by-faith salvation. As we have seen, τοῦτο regularly takes a conceptual antecedent. Whether faith is seen as a gift here or anywhere else in the NT is not addressed by this.
>
> A fourth view is that καὶ τοῦτο is adverbial, though this view has surprisingly made little impact on the exegetical literature. If adverbial, καὶ τοῦτο is intensive, meaning "and at that, and especially," without having any antecedent. It focuses on the *verb* rather than on any noun. In 3 John 5 we see this usage: πιστὸν ποιεῖς ὃ ἐὰν ἐργάσῃ εἰς τοὺς ἀδελφοὺς καὶ τοῦτο ξένους ("you do a faithful [deed] whenever you render service for the brothers, **and especially** [when you do it] for strangers"). If this is the force in Eph 2:8, the text means "for by grace you are saved through

faith, **and** [you are saved] **especially** not by your own doing; it is the gift of God."

The issues here are complex and cannot be solved by grammar alone. Nevertheless, syntactical considerations do tend toward one of the latter two views.[2]

The following discussion will take a closer look at each of the four "standard interpretations." The third view will be reserved for last, because it provides a useful springboard into further discussion.

First and Second Views: Χάριτί or Πίστεως as Antecedents

Both sides of the argument on *faith* as the antecedent predate the Reformation.[3] While some commentators and theologians argue for *faith* as the antecedent,[4] it has been roundly rejected for the reasons that Wallace mentions, both within Reformed circles and

---

[2] Daniel B. Wallace, *Greek Grammar Beyond the Basics: An Exegetical Syntax of the New Testament* (Grand Rapids: Zondervan, 1996), 334–35.

[3] S. T. Bloomfield, ῾Η Καινη Διαθηκη. *The Greek Testament with English Notes, Critical, Philological, and Exegetical*, 2nd ed., vol. 2 (London: n.p., n.d.; reprint, Philadelphia: Lippincott, 1860), 267–68, quotes Theophylact in support of *salvation* as the antecedent, and says that Chrysostom held the same position. He did not; he quite explicitly states that *faith* is the antecedent in *Homilies on the Epistles of St. Paul the Apostle to the Galatians and Ephesians*, Oxford translation revised and annotated by Gross Alexander, in *Nicene and Post-Nicene Fathers*, ed. Philip Schaff, first series, vol. 13, *Chrysostom: Homilies on Galatians, Ephesians, Philippians, Colossians, Thessalonians, Timothy, Titus, and Philemon*, American ed. (N.p.: Christian Literature, 1889; reprint, Peabody, MA: Hendrickson, 1995), 67.

[4] *The New Testament of our Lord Jesus Christ* (London: Barker, 1602); reprinted as *The Geneva Bible (The Annotated New Testament, 1602 edition)*, ed. Gerald T. Sheppard (New York: Pilgrim, 1989), 108; John Gill, *Romans to Revelation*, Commentary on the Old and New Testaments, vol. 6 (London: Hill, 1854; reprint, Grand Rapids: Baker, 1980), 427; George Barlow, *Galatians, Ephesians, Philippians, Colossians and I.–II. Thessalonians*, Preacher's Complete Homiletic Commentary, vol. 29 (New York: Funk & Wagnalls, n.d.), 154; Lewis Sperry Chafer, *The Ephesian Letter Doctrinally Considered* (New York: Loizeaux, 1935), 79; Charles Hodge, *A Commentary on the Epistle to the Ephesians* (New York: Carter, 1856; reprint, Grand Rapids: Baker, 1982), 118; E. K. Simpson, "Commentary on the Epistle to the Ephesians," in *Commentary on the Epistles to the Ephesians and Colossians* by E. K. Simpson and F. F. Bruce, New International Commentary on the New Testament, ed. Ned B. Stonehouse (Grand Rapids: Eerdmans, 1975), 54–55.

without.⁵ It is noteworthy that even many Reformed commentators reject it on grammatical grounds, despite their theological belief that faith is, in fact, a gift from God.⁶

MacArthur attempts a solution to the gender problem:

> Our response in salvation is **faith**, but even that is **not of yourselves** [but is] **the gift of God**. . . .
> Some have objected to this interpretation, saying that **faith** (*pistis*) is feminine, while **that** (*touto*) is neuter. That poses no problem, however, as long as it is understood that **that** does not refer precisely to the noun **faith** but to the act of believing. Further, this interpretation makes the best sense of the text. . . .⁷

MacArthur does not distinguish between a single-word and a conceptual (multiple-word) antecedent. With certain exceptions (see further discussion below), the demonstrative pronoun and its single-word antecedent agree in gender. No such agreement is required for conceptual (multiple-word) antecedents, since such an antecedent often contains nouns of more than one gender, as well as genderless words (e.g., finite verbs). *Sans* any validation whatsoever, this explanation posits a conceptual antecedent (thereby lifting the gender-agreement requirement) represented by a single word—a category of usage unheard of in the Pauline corpus. Thus while seeking to avoid special pleading in the

---

⁵ T. K. Abbott, *A Critical and Exegetical Commentary on the Epistles to the Ephesians and to the Colossians*, The International Critical Commentary on the Holy Scriptures of the Old and New Testaments, ed. Samuel Rolles Driver, Alfred Plummer, and Charles Augustus Briggs (Edinburgh: Clark, 1897), 51; John R. W. Stott, *The Message of Ephesians: God's New Society*, The Bible Speaks Today, ed. John R. W. Stott (Leicester and Downers Grove, IL: Inter-Varsity, 1979), 83; Randolph O. Yeager, *The Renaissance New Testament*, vol. 14 (Gretna, LA: Pelican, 1983), 218–19; Ernest Best, *A Critical and Exegetical Commentary on Ephesians*, International Critical Commentary on the Holy Scriptures of the Old and New Testaments (Edinburgh: Clark, 1998), 226.

⁶ E.g., Calvin, 227; Stott, *Message of Ephesians*, 83; Yeager, *Renaissance New Testament*, vol. 14, 218–19; Best, *Ephesians*, 226.

⁷ John F. MacArthur, Jr., *Ephesians*, MacArthur New Testament Commentary (Chicago: Moody Press, 1986), 60–61.

matter of gender, MacArthur makes an even greater special pleading. He may at least claim illustrious company: Darby appears to hold the same view, among others.[8]

Countess also expends considerable effort on the matter of gender here, and adduces three arguments. First, he argues that the gender of language is artificial, since it only partially corresponds to gender in the physical world. This is obviously true. From this premise, he continues:

> For example in Greek, "house" is sexless, but may be denoted by either the masculine οἶκός; or the feminine οἰκία. On the other hand, gender is *partially* linked to sex—e.g., names of male human beings, designations of male kinship relations such as "uncle," designations of occupations usually performed by men are modified by masculine adjectival forms. In view of this, one should not be surprised to find that where grammatical gender and physical sex conflict, *the gender of a pronoun may sometimes agree with the physical sex of its antecedent rather than the grammatical gender*.
> Returning to the case in point, one may observe that since both πίστις and τοῦτο are sexless, Paul would violate no propriety of physical gender at all by referring back to faith with τοῦτο instead of αὕτη.[9]

Countess is undoubtedly correct that referring to faith in the neuter "would violate no propriety of physical gender." Unfortunately, *that is not the point*. It does violate certain proprieties—or at least high probabilities—of *grammatical* gender, which, as Countess has already (correctly) established, has only a *partial* correspondence with physical gender, and therefore cannot be judged by the norms of physical gender. Referring to

---

[8] J. N. Darby, *Synopsis of the Books of the Bible*, vol. 4, *Acts–Philippians* (New York: Loizeaux, n.d.; reprint, Oak Park, IL: Bible Truth, 1970), 399; Robert Jamieson, A. R. Fausset, and David Brown, *Commentary Practical and Explanatory on the Whole Bible*, rev. ed. (Grand Rapids: Zondervan, 1961), 1284; William Hendricksen, *Exposition of Ephesians*, New Testament Commentary (Grand Rapids: Baker, 1967), 122–23. Also see discussion of Countess' third argument, page 82.

[9] Robert H. Countess, "Thank God for the Genitive," *Journal of the Evangelical Theological Society* 12 (Spring 1969): 119.

οἰκίᾳ with οὗτος or to οἶκός with αὕτη would also violate no proprieties of physical gender, but it would be ridiculous nonetheless.

Countess' second argument is based on πίστις as the nearer antecedent to τοῦτο. The problem with the so-called "rule of the nearer antecedent" is that it simply does not exist, as numerous grammarians will attest. Zerwick offers a delightful example:

> Thus e.g. Peter before the Sanhedrin after the cure of the lame man, having spoken of Christ «whom God has raised from the dead», goes on: «ἐν τούτῳ οὗτος stands before you cured. Οὗτος is the stone that was rejected . . .» (Acts 4,10f). This last οὗτος here refers back to the same antecedent as ἐν τούτῳ, i. e. Christ, an antecedent remote in the grammatical sense but proximate in the speaker's mind as being the subject of the whole discourse.[10]

Winer summarizes the issue thus:

> The pronoun οὗτος sometimes refers, not to the noun which stands nearest to it, but to one more remote, which is to be regarded as the principal subject, and which therefore was to the writer the nearest *psychologically*,—was more vividly present to his mind than any other.[11]

Turner agrees: ". . . not necessarily referring to the noun which is nearest, but to the noun which is most vividly in the writer's mind (deictic)."[12] Dana and Mantey concur.[13] Wallace adds that the "nearer" antecedent may be nearer "in the space or time of the

---

[10] Maximilian Zerwick, *Biblical Greek Illustrated by Examples*, trans. and adapted by Joseph Smith (Rome: Pontifical Bible Institute, 1963), 68.

[11] G. B. Winer, *A Treatise on the Grammar of the New Testament*, trans. W. F. Moulton (Edinburgh: Clark, 1882; reprint, Eugene, OR: Wipf and Stock, 1997), 195. Winer also offers a number of instructive examples.

[12] Nigel Turner, *Syntax*, vol. 3 of *A Grammar of New Testament Greek* (Edinburgh: Clark, 1963), 44.

[13] H. E. Dana and Julius R. Mantey, *A Manual Grammar of the Greek New Testament* (New York: Macmillan, 1927), 129.

writer or audience."[14] BDF offers not a word about the nearer antecedent of οὗτος.[15] Robertson also declines to address the nearness issue specifically, but makes an instructive comment: "Sometimes only the context can clear up the exact reference of the anaphoric οὗτος. So in Ac. 8:26 αὕτη points to ἡ ὁδὸς."[16]

Since the "nearer" antecedent is a matter of contextual definition and not merely a matter of counting the words between the pronoun and its putative antecedents, Countess would need to support this argument by discussing the context, which he does not. As the discussion below will demonstrate, the context does define a "nearer" antecedent—and πίστις is not it.

Countess' third argument comes closer to the point: he argues (quoting Kuyper) that "A *neutral* demonstrative pronoun is frequently used to refer to a preceding masculine or *feminine* noun, when the meaning expressed by the word is taken in a general sense."[17] Three examples follow, all drawn from classical—not *Koinē*—Greek. This in itself is a problem, the issue is whether the usage appears in *Koinē* (i.e., whether the usage was current when Paul wrote). Furthermore, one of the examples does not use οὗτος, the pronoun at issue, and of the remaining two that do, the latter arguably has a conceptual referent, leaving one clean example, not in the *Koinē* period. Notwithstanding

---

[14] Wallace, *Grammar*, 325–26.

[15] F. Blass and A. Debrunner, *A Greek Grammar of the New Testament and other Early Christian Literature*, trans. and rev. Robert W. Funk (Chicago: University of Chicago Press, 1961), 151.

[16] A. T. Robertson, *A Grammar of the Greek New Testament in the Light of Historical Research*, 4th ed. (New York: Hodder and Stoughton, 1923; reprint, Nashville, TN: Broadman, 1934), 698.

[17] Countess, "Thank God," 120. This contention appears to underlie MacArthur's argument (*Ephesians*, 60–61).

Countess' failure to demonstrate his case, two Pauline instances exist where (though unlikely) τοῦτο referring to a single-word feminine referent is not impossible.[18]

Wallace's critique is correct: understanding a neuter demonstrative pronoun to refer to the feminine noun *faith* would be an oddity, requiring considerable defense, and of course the same objections apply to *grace* (also feminine) as the antecedent. Either constitutes special pleading at best. As the discussion below will demonstrate, an unusual usage here is vanishingly unlikely.

Fourth View: Καὶ Τοῦτο as Adverbial with no Antecedent

Wallace's fourth option, translating καὶ τοῦτο as "and especially," would resolve the grammatical tension in the issue.[19] Suppose the verse did say, "For by grace you are saved through faith, *and especially* not of yourselves, it is the gift of God, not of works, lest anyone should boast." The theological contention would continue, but instead of arguing over the antecedent of τοῦτο, scholars would debate the identity of *the gift of God*.[20] If legitimate, this rendering would shift the grammatical detail at issue, because

---

[18] 2 Cor. 13:9 and Phil. 1:28 are arguable. In the former case, the question is whether τοῦτο refers back to the preceding elements Paul wishes for them (conceptual) or forward to κατάρτισιν (see Turner, *Syntax*, 45; Robertson, *Grammar*, 698, 703.) In the latter case, the question is whether τοῦτο refers to σωτηρίας or to a larger concept in the preceding context. Wallace, *Grammar*, 335; Best, *Ephesians*, 226, prefer a conceptual referent, and Homer A. Kent, Jr., "Philippians," in *Expositor's Bible Commentary*, ed. Frank E. Gaebelein, vol. 11, *Ephesians–Philemon* (Grand Rapids: Regency, 1978), 119, offers a useful suggestion for identifying the concept. See John Banker, *A Semantic and Structural Analysis of Philippians* (Dallas: SIL, 1996), 73, for further discussion.

[19] Turner, *Syntax*, 45; Walter Bauer, *A Greek-English Lexicon of the New Testament and Other Early Christian Literature*, rev. and ed. Frederick William Danker, 3rd ed. (Chicago: University of Chicago Press, 2000), 495, take this position.

[20] Identifying the gift of God is the real issue in any case. Theologians who argue for πίστεως (*faith*) as the antecedent of τοῦτο do so precisely because they want to identify *faith* as *the gift of God*.

the gender of the pronoun would no longer be a factor. One could then plausibly suggest that faith is the gift of God without the need to resort to special pleading.

However, this option suffers fatal difficulties. Even accepting Wallace's analysis of the construction, the adverbial use of καὶ τοῦτο would be rare, requiring considerable validation that it is, in fact, adverbial here. Furthermore, Wallace's case for this category is shaky at best. Three of his four examples have a clear conceptual referent, and the last one (problematic, but very possibly adverbial) is outside of Paul.[21] In fact, every neuter use of οὗτος in Pauline literature has a referent (usually conceptual) in the context.[22] Wallace appeals to a category of usage for τοῦτο which Paul simply does not evidence. While this option initially looks promising, ultimately, it only substitutes one special pleading for another. Further, it suffers from contextual difficulties, since a highly probable conceptual referent for τοῦτο exists in the context.[23]

Third View: "Grace-by-Faith Salvation" as Antecedent

Wallace's third option, that τοῦτο refers to the concept of "grace-by-faith salvation," comes closer to the mark. As noted above, one expects a multiple-word (i.e., conceptual) referent with a neuter form of οὗτος, the more so here since the context lacks

---

[21] In Rom. 13:11, τοῦτο refers to the commands listed in the preceding paragraph. In 1 Cor. 6:6 τοῦτο refers to the act discussed in the preceding clause, ἀδελφὸς μετὰ ἀδελφοῦ κρίνεται. In 1 Cor. 6:8 τοῦτο (ταῦτα in the Majority Text) refers to the actions listed in the preceding clause ὑμεῖς ἀδικεῖτε καὶ ἀποστερεῖτε. Wallace's non-Pauline example, 3 John 5, is likely adverbial, although other options are possible (note that this example does not appear in the Majority Text).

[22] Ann Marshall and Timothy R. Nichols, "Neuter Uses of Οὗτος in Paul" (paper submitted for 305 Advanced Greek Grammar, Chafer Theological Seminary, Fall 2000). Note also that Best, *Ephesians*, 226, cites Wallace's first three examples of the putative adverbial use (along with Phil. 1:28) in support of a conceptual referent in this construction.

[23] See discussion on page 87.

any neuter word that could plausibly be its referent. Of Wallace's four options, seeking a conceptual referent is by far the best choice.

A conceptual referent does not simply appear out of the æther; rather, it is a group of words in the immediate context.[24] One must therefore ask the question, "What group of words does Paul have in mind here?" Wallace's third option would answer, "Χάριτί ἐστε σεσῳσμένοι διὰ τῆς πίστεως (*by grace you are saved through faith*)."[25]

Hoehner offers a slight variation on this theme:

---

[24] Under the heading "Conceptual Antecedent/Postcedent," Wallace, *Grammar*, 333, says, "The neuter of οὗτος is routinely used to refer to a phrase or clause." Harold W. Hoehner, "Ephesians," in *The Bible Knowledge Commentary*, ed. John F. Walvoord and Roy B. Zuck, vol. 2, *New Testament* (Wheaton, IL: Victor, 1983), 624, notes that τοῦτο is used in precisely this way in 1:15 and 3:1.

[25] See Best, *Ephesians*, 226–27; Gregory P. Sapaugh, "Is Faith a Gift? A Study of Ephesians 2:8," *Journal of the Grace Evangelical Society* 7 (Spring 1994): 39; Ralph P. Martin, "Ephesians," in *New Bible Commentary*, 3rd ed., edited by D. Guthrie and J. A. Motyer (Leicester: Inter-Varsity; Grand Rapids, Eerdmans, 1970), 1110; William MacDonald, *Believer's Bible Commentary: Old and New Testaments*, ed. Art Farstad (Nashville, TN: Nelson, 1995), 1918; Homer A. Kent, Jr., *Ephesians: The Glory of the Church* (Chicago: Moody Press, 1971), 39; Karl Braune, *The Epistle of Paul to the Ephesians*, trans. with additions, M. B. Riddle, A Commentary on the Holy Scriptures: Critical, Doctrinal, and Homiletical, with Special Reference to Ministers and Students, ed. John Peter Lange, (series) translated and edited, Philip Schaff, New Testament, vol. 7 (Edinburgh: Clark, 1870; reprint, Grand Rapids: Zondervan, 1960), 80 (perhaps); Stott, *Message of Ephesians*, 83; Abbott, *Ephesians*, 51; Max Anders, *Galatians, Ephesians, Philippians & Colossians*, Holman New Testament Commentary, ed. Max Anders (Nashville, TN: Broadman & Holman, 1999), 112; Andrew T. Lincoln, *Ephesians*, Word Biblical Commentary, ed. David A. Hubbard and Glenn W. Barker, vol. 42 (Dallas: Word, 1990), 112; J. Vernon McGee, *Thru the Bible with J. Vernon McGee*, vol. 5 (Pasadena, CA: Thru the Bible Radio, 1983), 236–37 (apparently); C. Leslie Mitton, *Ephesians*, New Century Bible Commentary, ed. Matthew Black. (London: Marshall, Morgan, and Scott, 1973; paperback reprint, London: Marshall, Morgan, and Scott; Grand Rapids: Eerdmans, 1981), 96–97; Archibald Thomas Robertson, *Word Pictures in the New Testament*, vol. 4, *The Epistles of Paul* (Nashville, TN: Broadman, 1931), 525 (apparently); S. D. F. Salmond, "The Epistle to the Ephesians," in *The Expositor's Greek New Testament*, ed. W. Robertson Nicoll, vol. 3 (Grand Rapids: Eerdmans, 1961), 289 (apparently); Willard H. Taylor, "Ephesians," in *Beacon Bible Commentary*, ed. A. F. Harper, et al., vol. 9 (Kansas City, MO: Beacon Hill, 1969), 173 (apparently); Harold F. Pellegrin, *The Epistle of Paul the Apostle to the Ephesians: Studies in the Christian Life* (Grand Rapids: Zondervan, 1937), 179; F. F. Bruce, *The Epistles to the Colossians, to Philemon, and to the Ephesians*, New International Commentary on the New Testament, ed. F. F. Bruce (Grand Rapids: Eerdmans, 1984), 289–90; Bloomfield, *The Greek Testament*, vol. 2, 267–68; A. Skevington Wood, "Ephesians," in *Expositor's Bible Commentary*, edited by Frank E. Gaebelein, vol. 11, *Ephesians–Philemon* (Grand Rapids: Regency, 1978), 36–37; "Ephesians," in *NIV Bible Commentary*, ed. Kenneth L. Barker and John R. Kohlenberger, III, vol. 2, *New Testament* (Grand Rapids: Zondervan, 1994), 758–59. Many commentators unfortunately refer to the concept of salvation without referencing the Greek words directly, but a conceptual referent always rises from specific verbiage in the text.

Rather than any particular word it is best to conclude that τοῦτο refers back to the preceding section. This is common and there are numerous illustrations of such in Ephesians. For example, in 1:15 τοῦτο refers back to the contents of 1:3–14, in 3:1 it refers back to 2:11–22, and in 3:14 it refers back to 3:1–13. Therefore, in the present context, τοῦτο refers back to 2:4–8a and more specifically to 2:8a, the concept of salvation by grace through faith.[26]

MacArthur objects to the third option:

> . . . if **that** refers to **by grace you have been saved through faith** (that is, to the whole statement), the adding of **and that not of yourselves, it is the gift of God** would be redundant, because grace is defined as an unearned act of God.[27]

MacArthur would have his readers believe that Paul would not refer to the whole of 2:8a because the very word *grace*, by definition, already makes the point. However, Paul has never been shy about driving a point home through repetition, particularly antithetical repetition. Furthermore, one must ask, "How do we *know* that 'grace is defined as an unearned act of God'?" The definition of *grace* is not carved on the hearts of all men from the moment of birth; it was not engraved on golden plates and given to men by an angel; the inspired Scriptures do not come with an inspired glossary. No, God reveals the definition of *grace* by what He says about *grace*—in passages just like this one.

If there were no more context than 2:8–9 provides, taking the whole of 2:8a as the referent of τοῦτο would be entirely plausible. However, since the sentence in 2:8–9 begins with γὰρ, one must take account of the immediately preceding sentence (2:1–7) to which it connects. Once that is done, even the third view requires modification.

---

[26] Hoehner, *Ephesians*, 342–43.

[27] MacArthur, *Ephesians*, 61.

FINDING THE CORRECT CONCEPTUAL REFERENT

Some commentators take τοῦτο to refer to the periphrastic ἐστε σεσῳσμένοι (*you are saved*).[28] Others put forward salvation as the referent for τοῦτο, without citing the specific words involved.[29] Hendricksen objects to the latter approach, saying (specifically of Robertson), ". . . he should have justified the departure from the rule that unless there is a compelling reason to do otherwise the antecedent should be looked for in the immediate vicinity of the pronoun or adjective that refers to it."[30] Hendricksen is partly right: the conceptual referent is a *multiple-word* referent: one cannot simply posit an idea as antecedent without grounding it in actual words in the context. But which words?

Paul's own summary of his main thought in 2:1–7 is χάριτί ἐστε σεσῳσμένοι (*by grace you are saved*). Paul reintroduces this clause at the beginning of 2:8 (as his continuing topic of discussion) to add the new information that by-grace salvation occurs

---

[28] John Eadie, *A Commentary on the Greek Text of the Epistle of Paul to the Ephesians*, ed. W. Young (Edinburgh: Clark, 1883; reprint, Grand Rapids: Baker, 1979), 152

[29] Alfred Martin, "Ephesians," in *Wycliffe Bible Commentary*, ed. Charles F. Pfeiffer and Everett F. Harrison (Chicago: Moody Press, 1962), 1306; Henry F. Alford, *The Greek New Testament*, vol. 3, *Galatians–Philemon*, rev. Everett F. Harrison (Chicago: Moody Press, 1968), 94; Francis W. Beare and Theodore O. Wedel, "The Epistle to the Ephesians," in *Interpreter's Bible*, ed. George Arthur Buttrick, vol. 10 (New York: Abingdon, 1953), 644; Calvin, *Galatians and Ephesians*, 227–28; Robertson, *Grammar*, 704 (apparently, although *Word Pictures*, vol. 4, 525 would seem to argue otherwise); R. C. H. Lenski, *The Interpretation of St. Paul's Epistles to the Galatians, to the Ephesians and to the Philippians* (Minneapolis, MN: Augsburg, 1937), 423; Ralph P. Martin, "Ephesians," in *2 Corinthians–Philemon*, The Broadman Bible Commentary, ed. Clifton J. Allen, vol. 11 (Nashville, TN: Broadman, 1971), 143; Pheme Perkins, "Ephesians," in *2 Corinthians–Philemon*, New Interpreter's Bible, ed. Leander E. Keck, et al., vol. 11 (Nashville: Abingdon, 2000), 392; Jim Townsend, "'Saved By Grace Alone—This is All my Plea' (An Exposition of Ephesians 2:8–10)," *Emmaus Journal* 7 (Winter 1998); electronic reprint (Garland, TX: Galaxie, 2002), 235–36; Marvin R. Vincent, *Word Studies in the New Testament*, vol. 3, *The Epistles of Paul* (New York: Scribner, 1890; reprint, Grand Rapids: Eerdmans, 1946), 376.

[30] Hendricksen, *Ephesians*, 121.

διὰ τῆς πίστεως (*through faith*). The continuing topic of discussion, then, is χάριτί ἐστε σεσῳσμένοι, i.e., by-grace salvation.[31] There being no neuter word in the context that fits, readers would look for a prior conceptual referent when Paul opens a new clause with καὶ τοῦτο. A clause repeated twice in the immediate context as the continuing topic of discussion would be impossible to miss[32] (see graphic below).[33]

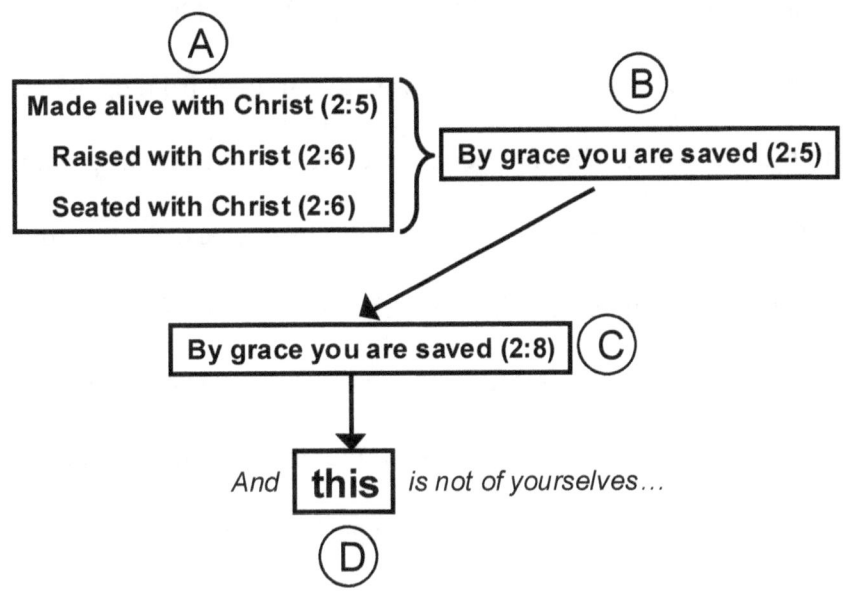

---

[31] Max Turner, "Ephesians," in *New Bible Commentary*, 4th ed., edited by G. J. Wenham, J. A. Motyer, D. A. Carson, and R. T. France (Leicester and Downers Grove, IL: Inter-Varsity, 1994), 1230, appears to agree: "The salvation . . . is not the product of, nor the reward given to, our works; it is *the gift of God* to faith. (Paul's Greek does not suggest that he is saying that the faith too is purely by God's grace, though that may be implied by other considerations.)" Alexander MacLaren, *Expositions of Holy Scripture*, vol. 13, *Ephesians* (London: Hodder and Stoughton, 1909; reprint, Grand Rapids: Baker, 1974), 105, also agrees, although on rather shaky grounds.

[32] Eadie, *Ephesians*, 151–52, argues similarly.

[33] The graphic represents a simplification of the grammatical diagram. Pages 17–18 give a complete grammatical diagram of the passage.

As the graphic shows, D refers to C, which repeats B, which summarizes A. Throughout the context Paul has maintained his emphasis on by-grace salvation: it is his continuous topic. Χάριτί ἐστε σεσῳσμένοι (*by grace you are saved*), then, is the antecedent of τοῦτο. This by-grace salvation is not from man's effort; it is God's gift, not accomplished by works, which precludes any boasting.

CONCLUSION

After two millennia of various traditions muddying the waters, the search for the antecedent of τοῦτο seems quite a puzzle. But Paul has provided clear markers in the text to emphasize his topic, and when we turn our eyes from the wind and waves of tradition to the Word itself, the antecedent becomes clear. Both the grammar and Pauline usage discount a simple reference to χάριτί or πίστεως, and Pauline usage likewise discounts the adverbial rendering, which leaves a conceptual referent as the best possibility. Even were the other options more viable, one must ask what the most likely referent might be, and again the answer is a conceptual referent in the immediate context. If the conceptual referent were as broad as Wallace suggests, Τῇ γὰρ χάριτί ἐστε σεσῳσμένοι διὰ τῆς πίστεως (*by grace you are saved through faith*), then one might argue (although not without some resistance) that all the items within it (including faith) are gifts of God. However, Paul's repetition of χάριτί ἐστε σεσῳσμένοι (*by grace you are saved*) makes his antecedent clear. Thus those who would understand faith as a divine gift find no succor in this context. If the evidence can be found at all, it will be in other passages, not in this one.

CHAPTER 7

CONCLUSION

SUMMARY

Paul opens his epistle by telling his Gentile audience to praise the Father (1) for His role in planning and preparing the salvation of the Jews, to the praise of the glory of His grace, (2) for the Son's role in carrying out the salvation of the Jews, to the praise of the Father's glory—in which salvation the Gentile believers also partake—and (3) for the Spirit's role in securing the destiny of Gentile and Jewish believers, to the praise of the Father's glory. He then offers a prayer that God, having already begun to enlighten his readers, would reveal to them the certain end to which He called them, the rich inheritance He lays up for them, and His great power that works in them—the same power that raised Christ from the dead and set Him over everything and everyone.

In the passage at hand in this study, Paul plumbs the depths of his Gentile readers' former situation, not sparing himself and his Jewish fellow-believers the same searching examination, and coming to the same conclusion for both: all were spiritually dead and wallowing in that state. However, Paul has prayed that God would enlighten his readers as to how the same power that raised Christ from the dead and seated Him in the heavenlies works in them, and he seeks an answer to that prayer. Despite the loathsome former state of both Gentile and Jewish believers, Paul explains, God united them together with Christ, making them alive with Him, raising them with Him, and seating them with Him in the heavenlies—that is, He saved them by grace. Furthermore, this by-grace salvation in all its parts, including regeneration, appropriates to the individual through faith, not works. One has only to believe, and he is united with Christ, and thereby given spiritual life and all else that union entails. Of necessity, then, the spiritually dead man believes—indeed, must believe—for only then is he made spiritually alive. Such a salvation cannot be earned by works; it is God's gift, which precludes any human boasting, because believers collectively are God's single work, created in Christ for the Father's preplanned purposes.

While minor exegetical skirmishes are being fought in Ephesians 2:1–10, the major points on which the argument of the passage depends are not significantly contested. And those points lead directly to this conclusion: one enters into regeneration and all the other fruits of identification with Christ through the doorway of faith—not *vice versa*, as Reformation theology would have it. *Theologia semper reformanda est.*

AREAS FOR FURTHER STUDY

This study has presented one example of the hazards that inhere in taking a "system first; texts afterward" approach to interpreting Scripture. Both Calvinist and Arminian systems perpetuate a major problem by understanding faith and spiritual death as mutually exclusive by nature. (The Arminian need for the notion of prevenient grace demonstrates, but does not substantially change, the nature of the problem.) Ephesians 2:1–10 establishes that faith does occur before regeneration, and therefore for Calvinists demands a revision to the definition of at least one term, and perhaps both. Merely positing that faith is a gift from God hardly offers a resolution, since on the Reformed conception of spiritual death, a dead man *could neither receive nor benefit from such a gift*. Moreover, on the Reformed conception of faith as an act of the whole person (*notitia*, *assensus*, and *fiducia*), a dead man would never choose to exercise for good any ability to believe which God might grant him.

The demand on Arminians is less strenuous, but while the passage offers no explicit refutation of prevenient grace, neither does it offer support. The juxtaposition of the Arminian *ordo salutis* and the Arminian definition of spiritual death creates a theological dilemma. Prevenient grace is the putative solution. By contrast, Paul seems neither to notice the dilemma, nor to feel any need to explain *his* juxtaposition of spiritual death and the *ordo salutis* of Ephesians 2:1–10—which makes one wonder whether any dilemma exists. If not, then the Arminian definitions of death and faith require a second look as well, and current formulations of prevenient grace may well fall victim to William of Occam's famous blade.

In keeping with that demand, one of the most necessary areas of further study will be a truly *exegetical* look at the nature of spiritual death in a number of passages like this one, where major issues may have been overlooked. There will also be a need for quality exegesis of a number of passages having to do with the origin and nature of faith.[1] However, just as this passage does not determine the meaning of those others, neither do they determine the meaning of this one. These other passages are important, but if the argument of this thesis is wrong, it must be proven wrong *in Ephesians 2:1–10*.[2]

Resultant to those and other pertinent exegetical studies, additional theological work will be required on the nature of spiritual death and faith. One of the relevant

---

[1] Among the passages adduced by various writers in connection with Ephesians 2:8 are John 6:44–45, 65; Acts 3:19; 5:31; 11:18; Rom. 12:3; Phil. 1:29; 3:9; 2 Tim. 2:25; and 2 Pet. 1:1.

[2] An engineer inspecting the Hoover Dam might respond in a variety of ways when informed of a crack in the Arizona side of the dam. However, "I just inspected the Nevada side, and there is nothing wrong there!" is *not* an appropriate or relevant response. Likewise, upon being informed that his *ordo salutis* encounters a problem in Ephesians 2:1–10, the Reformed theologian may respond in a variety of ways, but "There are no problems in Philippians 1:29" is inappropriate and irrelevant, even if true.

theological questions is if faith is indeed a capacity inherent in man, yet is not a work, how does it happen? Some maintain that faith can be an act of the will without being a work, but that view seems to have an inherent tension. A passive conception of faith is one possible resolution, and work is under way to investigate it, but more work needs to be done.[3]

---

[3] For more information on the passive faith view, see Benjamin B. Warfield, "On Faith in its Psychological Aspects," in *Studies in Theology* (New York: Oxford University Press, 1932; reprint, Carlisle, PA: Banner of Truth, 1988) 313–42; Joseph C. Dillow, *The Reign of the Servant Kings: A Study of Eternal Security and the Final Significance of Man*, 2nd ed. (Hayesville, NC: Schoettle, 1993) 276–82; Zane C. Hodges, *Absolutely Free! A Biblical Reply to Lordship Salvation* (Dallas: Redención Viva; Grand Rapids: Academie, 1989), 25–33; Robert N. Wilkin, *Confident in Christ: Living by Faith Really Works* (Irving, TX: Grace Evangelical Society, 1999), 5–15; David R. Anderson, "The Nature of Faith," *CTS Journal* 5 (October–December 1999): 2–26; Timothy R. Nichols, "Commands to Believe: An Objection to Passive Faith?" paper presented to the National Teaching Pastors' Conference, Omaha, NE, October 2001; Stephen L. Andrew, "PROPER: a Free-Grace Alternative to Calvinism's TULIP and Arminianism's PEARS," paper presented to the National Teaching Pastors' Conference, Omaha, NE, October 2001; Timothy R. Nichols, "Is Faith a Decision?" paper presented to the National Teaching Pastors' Conference, San Juan Capistrano, CA, March 2002; Bruce Bumgardner, "Obedience/Disobedience to the Gospel: Is the Will Involved in Faith?" paper presented to the National Teaching Pastors' Conference, San Juan Capistrano, CA, March 2003.

APPENDIX 1
BAR OUTLINING

INTRODUCTION

This author used the BAR exegetical outlining method[1] in preparing this thesis. Since the method is largely unknown, some discussion is appropriate. A brief history of the BAR method will be followed by a sketch of its key principles. Finally, this appendix will discuss the application of the principles in the practice of the method.

PROVENANCE

The BAR method is a development of the "Pedantic Exegetical Outlining Method" developed and taught by Dr. Dale Wheeler, who developed it at Dallas Theological Seminary and continues to teach it today. The BAR method owes two key insights to Haddon Robinson. First, Robinson realized that the complete answer to the question *What is this passage about?* is not a word or phrase but a *proposition*, a complete sentence. He calls this proposition the passage's *subject*. Likewise, the answer to the question *What does this passage say about its subject?* is a proposition, which Robinson calls the passage's *complement*. Together, the *subject* and *complement* make up what Robinson terms the passage's *big idea*.[2] Second, Robinson understood that the *big idea* components must rise inductively out of the passage, not be forced on it by an enterprising homiletician.

---

[1] The acronym BAR stands for Boundary, Assertion, Relation.

[2] See Haddon W. Robinson, *Biblical Preaching: The Development and Delivery of Expository Messages* (Grand Rapids: Baker, 1980), 31–45. Note that the CTS New Testament Department has changed the terms *subject* and *complement* to *topic* and *comment*, respectively.

Wheeler realized that Haddon Robinson inductively derived the components of his *big idea* (i.e., the *subject* and *complement*) from the passage, but Robinson was unable to communicate to students how he accomplished this. Wheeler discovered that Robinson's (wholly intuitive) process depended on following structural markers, mostly conjunctions, in the text. Thus inspired, Wheeler developed a way of outlining a passage in keeping with its clause grammar that, when properly practiced, enables students to develop the *big idea* components inductively. During the time Wheeler taught his method as an instuctor at DTS, John Niemelä, then a Th.M. student, studied it under him and others. Recognizing its significance, Niemelä invested great time and effort in learning the method's intricacies in order to teach it himself, and he brought it with him to Chafer Theological Seminary. He has continued to fine-tune the method and its terminology, and has also made substantial improvements in the way it is transmitted to students. The author learned the method under Niemelä's tutelage in the fall of 1999 and the spring of 2000.[3]

PRINCIPLES

BAR outlines proceed upward from the bottom, that is, they begin with the lowest level of the outline and synthesize the next level up from the bottom-level points, and so forth.[4] Therefore, a BAR outline begins with the text and the grammatical diagram. The

---

[3] The author wrote his first paper presenting the method in the spring of 2000. A revised version appeared as "Reverse-Engineered Outlining: A Method for Epistolary Exegesis," *CTS Journal* 7 (April–June 2001): 16–58. At that time, CTS still used the terms *subject* and *complement*. The terminology caused confusion, because a given sentence would have not only a *semantic* subject and various complements, but also a *grammatical* subject and complement. A short time after the article appeared, Niemelä changed the semantic terms to *topic* and *comment*.

[4] See Appendix 2 for an example.

outline treats each element of the text in the order it appears in the text, and handles it according to its grammatical position in the sentence, as indicated by the diagram. Where options appear in the diagram, as they often do, the outline must reflect the interpreter's decision among the options.

Boundary

Each outline statement must reflect three overriding principles: Boundary, Assertion and Relation (hence the acronym BAR). Boundaries occur at all levels of a text, beginning with boundaries between words and proceeding to phrase boundaries, clause boundaries, sentence boundaries, paragraph boundaries, section boundaries, etc.[5] The boundary principle involves deciding how much text a given outline statement covers. For example, consider the text of Ephesians 1:4b–5a: εἶναι ἡμᾶς ἁγίους καὶ ἀμώμους κατενώπιον αὐτοῦ ἐν ἀγάπῃ προορίσας ἡμᾶς εἰς υἱοθεσίαν διὰ Ἰησοῦ Χριστοῦ εἰς αὐτόν (*that we be holy and blameless before Him in love having predestined us to adoption through Christ Jesus to Himself*). A clause-level statement covering 1:4b has to determine whether ἐν ἀγάπῃ (*in love*) modifies something in 1:4b or προορίσας (*having predestined*), that is, where does the boundary of the clause lie? In other words, does it read *that we be holy and blameless before Him in love; having predestined us to adoption*, or does it read *that we be holy and blameless before Him; in love having predestined us to adoption*? The diagram is no particular help here, as the grammar

---

[5] The categories listed by no means exhaust the possibilities. For example, the single sentence in Ephesians 1:3–14 has three parts (1:3–6, 7–12, 13–14), each smaller than a sentence and each larger than a clause.

permits either option. Defining the boundaries of a given block of text is prerequisite to making a statement about its meaning.⁶

Assertion

Assertion states the meaning of the text within the defined boundaries. Paraphrase is vital here, because "Bible-speak" can conceal a multitude of mutually exclusive interpretations. Verbal genitives provide a classic example of this phenomenon. Consider Paul's statement in 2 Corinthians 5:14: ἡ γὰρ ἀγάπη τοῦ Χριστοῦ συνέχει ἡμᾶς . . . (*For the love of Christ compels us . . .*). If an exegete were to paraphrase ἀγάπη τοῦ Χριστοῦ (*love of Christ*) by leaving in the *of*, one cannot discern the relationship between the words. Does *love of Christ* mean Paul's love for Christ, or Christ's love for Paul, or perhaps Christ's love for the lost? An assertion must not preserve the ambiguity: it should say exactly what the interpreter understands the text to mean, admitting no other interpretations (e.g., not *the love of Christ compels . . .*, but *Christ's love for the lost compels . . .*). Achieving such a paraphrase takes work, but permits better communication and rapid exposure of the locus of disagreement regarding the interpretation of a given text.

Relation

From Assertion one proceeds to Relation. To what in the context does the block of text at hand relate, and what is the nature of the relationship? A proper outline statement must include a clear statement that the block of text at hand relates to *x* block

---

⁶ Most outline statements contain material from outside the boundaries of the block of text at hand. In all such cases, the outside material appears in square brackets to signify that it is not part of the text under immediate consideration.

of text, and the nature of the relationship (cause, purpose, ground, time, inference, etc.) Relations can be equal-level (i.e., coordinate) or subordinate, and while a wide range of subordinate relations are possible, most are adverbial.

The Iterative Nature of BAR Principles

The BAR principles are iterative. In other words, while of course an exegete applies them at the lowest level (generally the clause level), the same principles apply at each higher level of the outline. Thus a sentence statement will acknowledge the sentence's boundaries, assert the sentence's meaning, and state its relation to the preceding sentence. Likewise, a paragraph statement will acknowledge the paragraph's boundaries, assert the paragraph's meaning, and state its relation to the preceding paragraph. The same holds true for units larger than a paragraph (e.g., Ephesians 1:3–3:21 and 4:1–6:20).

PRACTICE

The most nuanced grasp of the principles governing an exercise would be useless without concrete techniques for putting the principles into practice. Accordingly, the BAR method contains a specific set of conventions and distinctions to allow the exegete to apply its principles consistently. Two particular distinctions require elaboration: topic *versus* comment and signpost *versus* structural marker.

Topic **versus** *Comment*

Topic and comment describe a dependent relationship between two clauses. If Clause B depends upon Clause A, then Clause A is the *topic*, and clause B is the *comment* to Clause A (see diagram below).

```
_____Clause A_____
              |_____Clause B_____
```

One may have a topic without a comment, but never a comment without a topic. Note also that topic and comment are not entirely coextensive with independent and dependent clauses, respectively. Consider the example in the following diagram.

```
__Clause A (topic to B)__
       |__Clause B (comment to A; topic to C)__
                     |__Clause C (comment to B)__
```

Clause C depends on Clause B, and therefore Clause C is comment to Clause B. Likewise, Clause B is topic to Clause C. But Clause B is a *dependent clause*. It depends grammatically on clause A, and is comment to it. An independent clause is always a topic,[7] and a dependent clause is always a comment, but a dependent clause may also be topic to another clause that depends on it. Topic-comment relations reflect the clause structure of the text, as defined by the grammatical markers attached to clauses in the text.[8]

Signpost versus *Structural Marker*

Structural markers are the ligaments and tendons of the bottom (generally, clausal) level of the text. They hold various elements of the clause together and also

---

[7] This is true only in hypotactic sentence structure (e.g., Ephesians 2:1–10). In parataxis (e.g., Ephesians 4:26–27), independent clauses can function as comments due to logical (not grammatical) subordination.

[8] Again, this holds true in hypotactic sentence structure only. In paratactic structure, the author defines the clause relations logically rather than grammatically.

mark the relationship of a comment to its topic. The nature of the marker will indicate (within certain tolerances) the nature of the relationship between topic and comment.[9]

Signposts[10] link larger, equal-level units at the level of independent clause and higher. In other words, they link topic to topic. They can link sentence to sentence, or they can operate at a higher level. For example, the γάρ that begins Ephesians 2:10 links it to the preceding sentence. However, because the καὶ that begins Ephesians 2:1–10 begins a paragraph, it does not merely link sentence to sentence, but paragraph to paragraph (i.e., 2:1–10 to 1:15–23). In the same way, the οὖν in Ephesians 4:1 links 4:1–6:20 to 1:3–3:21, because it begins not only a paragraph, but a section.

Types of Outline Statements

A well-formed outline statement recognizes the boundaries of the block of text it interprets, contains an assertion of the meaning within those boundaries in as exact as possible a paraphrase, and states its relations to propositions outside its boundaries. Accordingly, there are three basic types of outline statement: topic statements, topic-to-topic statements, and topic-to-comment statements. If the block of text at hand is a topic unconnected to other topics, then it is the first type. This type is unaffected by the relationship principle of BAR, since it relates to nothing prior in the text. A simple statement of its meaning suffices. This is also the least common type of statement.

---

[9] The particular structural marker in the text limits the range of potential relations, although most structural markers have more than one possible meaning. E.g., ὅτι may indicate a content or causal relation, but never a purpose relation.

[10] Signposts are usually coordinating conjunctions appearing at the head of a sentence.

Most topics connect to some preceding topic by means of a signpost. In such a case, the interpreter summarizes the text at hand in a topic-to-topic statement that includes the following: (1) a statement of the preceding topic to which the text at hand relates (this appears in square brackets because it is outside the boundaries of the text at hand), (2) the nature of the relationship between the two topics, and (3) an assertion of the meaning of the topic at hand. Topic-to-topic statements are more common in the upper levels of the outline.

A comment statement never appears by itself, because every comment relates to a topic. If the block of text at hand is a comment, then the exegete summarizes it in a topic-to-comment statement, which states the topic to which it relates (in square brackets), the nature of the relationship, and an assertion of the comment's meaning. The topic-to-comment statement is by far the most common type of outline statement.

Sentence Structure in Outline Statements

In every case, the outline statement is a complete sentence, and it is always only one sentence, even though the sentence may be inordinately long. This forces the exegete to articulate the relationship between each part of the text under discussion in the statement. When outlining high-level points, for example, the outline statement covering Ephesians 1:3–3:21, the temptation to insert a sentence break can be acute, but it must be resisted at all costs. The temptation is so acute precisely because the exegete does not know how to relate the two parts of the statement. A sentence break with no conjunction to mark its relation to the preceding sentence allows a great deal of ambiguity, and it is precisely that ambiguity the exegete must avoid.

CONCLUSION

Any serious student of the Word acknowledges that context must be the ultimate arbiter of meaning, and that an interpretation ought therefore to take very close account of the context. However, in practice, many expositors base their interpretation on an intuitive leap to a conclusion regarding the main topic of the passage, and then proceed to relate the details of the passage to their "big idea" in a top-down fashion. A correct procedure is the exact reverse. If the text is seeking to communicate, then it has an argument, and therefore a "big idea." But the "big idea" existed in the author's mind, and is transmitted to the readers only via the details of the text. Therefore, a reader must begin with the details of the text, synthesizing them together from the bottom upward to recreate (i.e., reverse-engineer)[11] the "big idea" intended by the author, always keeping each detail of the text in its proper relation to every other detail. The BAR method provides a concrete set of techniques to aid an interpreter in doing just that.

---

[11] CTS began to use the terminology *reverse-engineer* to describe this process shortly before the publication of Nichols, "Reverse-Engineered Outlining" in 2001.

APPENDIX 2

FULL OUTLINE OF EPHESIANS 2:1–10

1A. (1:1–2)
2A. (1:3–3:20)
   1B. (1:3–14)
   2B. (1:15–23)
   3B. Based on [his just-completed prayer that God will reveal to the Ephesians the greatness of His power that works in them (the power that raised Christ from the dead and seated Him in the heavenlies)], Paul explains that God made Jewish and Gentile believers alive together with Christ, and raised them together with Christ, and seated them together with Christ, that is, He saved them by grace (even though they were both spiritually dead and were living accordingly, and were both under His wrath) because of His love-motivated mercy, in order that He might display His grace, and the means by which they were saved by grace is through faith, and by implication, by-grace salvation is God's work and man cannot boast about it, because God created the church as His corporate (singular) creation in Christ for the purpose of doing the good works that He prepared for it (2:1–10).
      1C. Based on [his just-completed prayer that God will reveal the greatness of His power (the power that raised Christ from the dead and seated Him in the heavenlies) to the Ephesians], Paul explains that God made both Jewish and Gentile believers alive together with Christ, and raised them together with Christ, and seated them together with Christ, that is, He saved them by grace (even though both Jews and Gentiles were dead in their sins and under His wrath), because of His love-motivated mercy, in order that He might display His grace (2:1–7).
         1D. [God saved Jewish and Gentile believers by grace] although the Gentile believers were (once) spiritually dead and lived in a worldly and satanic manner, and Jewish believers also formerly lived among unbelievers in a fleshly manner, and were under God's wrath because of their sinful nature, just like the Gentile believers were (2:1–3).
            1E. [ὄντας ὑμᾶς] [God made Gentile believers alive together with Christ, raised them together with Christ, and seated them together with Christ], even though they were spiritually dead in their trespasses and sins (2:1).
            2E. [ποτε περιεπατήσατε] The manner in which the Gentile believers formerly lived was in sin according to this world and according to Satan, who works in the disobedient (that is, in unbelievers) (2:2).
            3E. [καὶ ἡμεῖς ... ποτε] Jewish believers also formerly lived among [the disobedient] (2:3a).
            4E. [ἐν ... ποιοῦντες] The manner in which [Jewish believers formerly lived among the disobedient] was in their flesh's passions, doing the flesh's and the mind's desires (2:3b).

103

- 5E. [καὶ] In addition to [living among the disobedient], Jewish believers were also once naturally recipients of (divine) wrath, just like the rest (of the disobedient) (2:3c).
- 2D. God made both Jewish and Gentile believers alive together with Christ, and raised them together with Christ, and seated them together with Christ, that is, He saved them by grace, because His great love causes Him to be merciful, in order that He might display His grace (2:4–7).
  - 1E. [δὲ] God [made Gentile believers and Jewish believers alive together with Christ, raised them together with Christ, and seated them together with Christ] (2:4a).
  - 2E. [ὢν] The reason [God made Gentile believers and Jewish believers alive together with Christ, raised them together with Christ, and seated them together with Christ] is because He is rich in mercy (2:4a).
  - 3E. [διὰ] The reason [God is rich in mercy] is because He loved Jewish (and Gentile) believers (2:4b).
  - 4E. [καὶ ὄντας] [God made Gentile and Jewish believers alive together with Christ, raised them together with Christ, and seated them together with Christ] although they were spiritually dead in sins (2:5a).
  - 5E. [συνεζωοποίησεν ... καὶ συνήγειρεν καὶ συνεκάθισεν] God made Jewish and Gentile believers alive together with Christ, raised them together with Christ, and seated them in the heavens together with Christ, that is, He saved Gentile (and Jewish) believers by grace (2:5b–6).
  - 6E. [ἵνα] The purpose for [God saving believers by grace] was in order that He might display His grace's overwhelming abundance in the coming ages by means of His kindness to believers (2:7).
- 2C. [γὰρ] In light of [God saving believers by grace in order to display grace], the means by which believers are saved by grace is through faith, and by implication salvation is not accomplished by man but given by God, in order that no one be able to boast about being saved by grace (2:8–9).
  - 1D. [χάριτί ἐστε σεσῳσμένοι] [God] saved believers by grace (2:8a).
  - 2D. [διὰ] The means by which [believers are saved by grace] is through faith (2:8a).
  - 3D. [καὶ τοῦτο] The implication of [salvation being by means of grace] is that salvation is not (accomplished) by man, but rather it is a gift from God, not something obtained through work (2:8b–9a).
  - 4D. [ἵνα μη] The purpose of [by-grace salvation being a gift] is in order that no one can boast (2:9b).
- 3C. The reason [no one can boast about being saved by grace] is because the church is corporately God's creation because He created it in Christ for the purpose of doing the good works that He prepared for it beforehand (2:10).
  - 1D. [γάρ] The reason [by-grace salvation is God's gift, which precludes human boasting] is because believers are corporately God's creation (2:10a).
  - 2D. [κτισθέντες] The reason [believers are corporately God's creation] is because God created them in Christ Jesus (2:10b).

3D. [ἐπὶ] The purpose [for God making believers into a single, corporate creation] is in order that they [corporately] might do good works (2:10b).

4D. [προητοίμασεν] God prepared [the good works believers are to do] beforehand in order that believers [corporately] should walk in them (2:10c).

BIBLIOGRAPHY

ORIGINAL SOURCES

The Greek New Testament. 4th ed. Edited by Barbara Aland, Kurt Aland, Johannes Karavidopoulos, Carlo M. Martini, and Bruce Metzger. Stuttgart: Bibelstiftung, 1993.

Hodges, Zane C., and Arthur L. Farstad, eds. *The Greek New Testament According to the Majority Text*. 2nd ed. Nashville, TN: Nelson, 1985.

Novum Testamentum Graece: Post Eberhard Nestle et Erwin Nestle. 27th ed. Edited by Barbara Aland, Kurt Aland, Johannes Karavidopoulos, Carlo M. Martini, and Bruce Metzger. Stuttgart: Bibelstiftung, 1993.

Robinson, Maurice A., and William G. Pierpont, eds. *The New Testament in the Original Greek According to the Byzantine/Majority Textform*. Roswell, GA: Original Word, 1991. Electronic reprint, Oak Harbor, WA: Logos Research Systems, 1995.

Tischendorf, Constantin, von, ed. *Novum Testamentum Graece*. 2 vols. Leipzig: Gieseke and Devrient, 1869–72. Reprint, Graz: Akademische, 1965.

Westcott, Brooke Foss, and Fenton John Anthony Hort, eds. *The New Testament in the Original Greek*. New York: Harper and Brothers, 1882. Reprint, New York: Macmillan, 1949.

COMMENTARIES

Abbott, T. K. *A Critical and Exegetical Commentary on the Epistles to the Ephesians and to the Colossians*. The International Critical Commentary on the Holy Scriptures of the Old and New Testaments, edited by Samuel Rolles Driver, Alfred Plummer, and Charles Augustus Briggs. Edinburgh: Clark, 1897.

Alford, Henry F. *The Greek New Testament*. Vol. 3, *Galatians–Philemon*. Revised by Everett F. Harrison. Chicago: Moody Press, 1968.

Anders, Max. *Galatians, Ephesians, Philippians & Colossians*. Holman New Testament Commentary, edited by Max Anders. Nashville, TN: Broadman and Holman, 1999.

Banker, John. *A Semantic and Structural Analysis of Philippians*. Dallas: SIL, 1996.

Barclay, William. *The Letters to the Galatians and Ephesians*. Revised ed. Daily Study Bible. Philadelphia: Westminster, 1976.

Barlow, George. *Galatians, Ephesians, Philippians, Colossians and I.–II. Thessalonians*. Preacher's Complete Homiletic Commentary, vol. 29. New York: Funk and Wagnalls, n.d.

Barth, Markus. *Ephesians: Introduction, Translation, and Commentary on Chapters 1–3*. The Anchor Bible, edited by William Foxwell Albright and David Noel Freedman, vol. 34. Garden City, NY: Doubleday, 1974.

Beare, Francis W., and Theodore O. Wedel. "The Epistle to the Ephesians." In *The Interpreters' Bible*, edited by George Arthur Buttrick, vol. 10, 597–749. New York: Abingdon, 1953.

Best, Ernest. *A Critical and Exegetical Commentary on Ephesians*. International Critical Commentary on the Holy Scriptures of the Old and New Testaments. Edinburgh: Clark, 1998.

Best, Ernest. "Dead in Trespasses and Sins (Eph. 2.1)." In *Essays on Ephesians*, 69–85. Edinburgh: Clark, 1997.

Bloomfield, S. T. *Ἡ Καινη Διαθηκη. The Greek Testament with English Notes, Critical, Philological, and Exegetical*. 2 vols. 2nd ed. London: n.p., n.d. Reprint of vol. 1, Boston: Perkins and Marvin, 1848; reprint of vol. 2, Philadelphia: Lippincott, 1860.

Braune, Karl. *The Epistle of Paul to the Ephesians*. Translated with additions by M. B. Riddle. A Commentary on the Holy Scriptures: Critical, Doctrinal, and Homiletical, with Special Reference to Ministers and Students, edited by John Peter Lange. (Series) translated and edited, Philip Schaff, New Testament, vol. 7. Edinburgh: Clark, 1870. Reprint, Grand Rapids: Zondervan, 1960.

Bruce, F. F. *The Epistles to the Colossians, to Philemon, and to the Ephesians*. The New International Commentary on the New Testament, edited by F. F. Bruce. Grand Rapids: Eerdmans, 1984.

Calvin, John. *Commentaries on the Epistles of Paul to the Galatians and Ephesians*. Translated by William Pringle. Edinburgh, Calvin Translation Society, n.d. Reprint, Grand Rapids, Baker, 1981.

Calvin, John. *Commentary on the Gospel According to John*. Vol. 1. Translated by William Pringle. Edinburgh, Calvin Translation Society, n.d. Reprint, Grand Rapids, Baker, 1981.

Chafer, Lewis Sperry. *The Ephesian Letter Doctrinally Considered*. New York: Loizeaux, 1935.

Chrysostom. *Homilies on the Epistles of St. Paul the Apostle to the Galatians and Ephesians.* Oxford translation revised and annotated by Gross Alexander. In *Nicene and Post-Nicene Fathers.* Edited by Philip Schaff. First Series, vol. 13, *Chrysostom: Homilies on Galatians, Ephesians, Philippians, Colossians, Thessalonians, Timothy, Titus, and Philemon.* American ed. N.p.: Christian Literature, 1889. Reprint, Peabody, MA: Hendrickson, 1995.

Darby, J. N. *Synopsis of the Books of the Bible.* Vol. 4, *Acts–Philippians.* New York: Loizeaux, n.d. Reprint, Oak Park, IL: Bible Truth, 1970.

Eadie, John. *A Commentary on the Greek Text of the Epistle of Paul to the Ephesians.* Edited by W. Young. Edinburgh: Clark, 1883. Reprint, Grand Rapids: Baker, 1979.

Gill, John. *Romans to Revelation.* Commentary on the Old and New Testaments, vol. 6. London: William Hill, 1854. Reprint, Grand Rapids: Baker, 1980.

Hendricksen, William. *Exposition of Ephesians.* New Testament Commentary. Grand Rapids: Baker, 1967.

Hodge, Charles. *A Commentary on the Epistle to the Ephesians.* New York: Carter, 1856. Reprint, Grand Rapids: Baker, 1982.

Hoehner, Harold W. "Ephesians." In *The Bible Knowledge Commentary*, edited by John F. Walvoord and Roy B. Zuck. Vol. 2, *New Testament*, 613–46. Wheaton, IL: Victor, 1983.

Hoehner, Harold W. *Ephesians: An Exegetical Commentary.* Grand Rapids: Baker Academic, 2002.

Hughes, R. Kent. *Ephesians: The Mystery of the Body of Christ.* Preaching the Word. Wheaton, IL: Crossway, 1990.

Hunter, Archibald M. *Galatians, Ephesians, Philippians, Colossians.* Layman's Bible Commentary, edited by Balmer H. Kelly, vol. 22. Richmond, VA: Knox, 1959.

Jamieson, Robert, A. R. Fausset, and David Brown. *Commentary Practical and Explanatory on the Whole Bible.* Revised ed. Grand Rapids: Zondervan, 1961.

Kent, Homer A., Jr. *Ephesians: The Glory of the Church.* Chicago: Moody Press, 1971.

Kent, Homer A., Jr. "Philippians." In *The Expositor's Bible Commentary*, edited by Frank E. Gaebelein, vol. 11, *Ephesians–Philemon*. 93–159. Grand Rapids: Regency, 1978.

Lenski, R. C. H. *The Interpretation of St. Paul's Epistles to the Galatians, to the Ephesians and to the Philippians.* Minneapolis, MN: Augsburg, 1937.

Lincoln, Andrew T. *Ephesians*. Word Biblical Commentary, edited by David A. Hubbard and Glenn W. Barker; New Testament, edited by Ralph P. Martin, vol. 42. Dallas: Word, 1990.

MacArthur, John F., Jr. *Ephesians*. MacArthur New Testament Commentary. Chicago: Moody Press, 1986.

MacDonald, William. *Believer's Bible Commentary: Old and New Testaments*. Edited by Art Farstad. Nashville, TN: Nelson, 1995.

MacLaren, Alexander. *Expositions of Holy Scripture*. Vol. 13, *Ephesians*. London: Hodder and Stoughton, 1909. Reprint, Grand Rapids: Baker, 1974.

Martin, Alfred. "Ephesians." In *Wycliffe Bible Commentary*. Edited by Charles F. Pfeiffer and Everett F. Harrison, 1301–17. Chicago: Moody Press, 1962.

Martin, Ralph P. "Ephesians." In *Broadman Bible Commentary*, edited by Clifton J. Allen, vol. 11, *2 Corinthians–Philemon*. 125–77. Nashville, TN: Broadman, 1971.

Martin, Ralph P. "Ephesians." In *New Bible Commentary*, 3rd ed. Edited by D. Guthrie and J. A. Moyer, 1105–124. Leicester: Inter-Varsity; Grand Rapids, Eerdmans, 1970.

McGee, J. Vernon. *Thru the Bible with J. Vernon McGee*, vol. 5. Pasadena, CA: Thru the Bible Radio, 1983.

Mitton, C. Leslie. *Ephesians*. New Century Bible Commentary. Edited by Matthew Black. London: Marshall, Morgan, and Scott, 1973. Paperback reprint, London: Marshall, Morgan, and Scott; Grand Rapids: Eerdmans, 1981.

The New Testament of our Lord Jesus Christ. London: Barker, 1602. Reprinted as *The Geneva Bible: (The Annotated New Testament, 1602 edition)*. Edited by Gerald T. Sheppard. New York: Pligrim, 1989.

Pellegrin, Harold F. *The Epistle of Paul the Apostle to the Ephesians: Studies in the Christian Life*. Grand Rapids: Zondervan, 1937.

Perkins, Pheme. "Ephesians." In *2 Corinthians–Philemon*. New Interpreter's Bible, edited by Leander E. Keck, et al., vol. 11. Nashville: Abingdon, 2000.

Robertson, Archibald Thomas. *Word Pictures in the New Testament*. Vol. 4, *The Epistles of Paul*. Nashville, TN: Broadman, 1931.

Salmond, S. D. F. "The Epistle to the Ephesians." In *The Expositor's Greek New Testament*, edited by W. Robertson Nicoll, vol. 3, 201–395. Grand Rapids: Eerdmans, 1961.

Simpson, E. K. "Commentary on the Epistle to the Ephesians." In *Commentary on the Epistles to the Ephesians and Colossians*. By E. K. Simpson and F. F. Bruce, The New International Commentary on the New Testament, edited by Ned B. Stonehouse, 8–157. Grand Rapids: Eerdmans, 1975.

Stott, John R. W. *The Message of Ephesians: God's New Society*. The Bible Speaks Today. Edited by John R. W. Stott. Leicester and Downers Grove, IL: Inter-Varsity, 1979.

Taylor, Willard H. "Ephesians." In *Beacon Bible Commentary*, edited by A. F. Harper, et al., vol. 9. Kansas City, MO: Beacon Hill, 1969.

Turner, Max. "Ephesians." In *New Bible Commentary*, 4th ed. Edited by G. J. Wenham, J. A. Moyer, D. A. Carson, and R. T. France, 1222–44. Leicester and Downers Grove, IL: Inter-Varsity, 1994.

Vincent, Marvin R. *Word Studies in the New Testament*. Vol. 3, *The Epistles of Paul*. New York: Scribner, 1890. Reprint, Grand Rapids: Eerdmans, 1946.

Wood, A. Skevington. "Ephesians." In *Expositor's Bible Commentary*, edited by Frank E. Gaebelein, vol. 11, *Ephesians–Philemon*. 1–92. Grand Rapids: Regency, 1978.

Wood, A. Skevington. "Ephesians." In *NIV Bible Commentary*, edited by Kenneth L. Barker and John R. Kohlenberger, III, vol. 2, *New Testament*, 748–86. Grand Rapids: Zondervan, 1994.

Yeager, Randolph O. *The Renaissance New Testament*, vol. 14. Gretna, LA: Pelican, 1983.

BOOKS

Arminius, James. "Certain Articles to be Diligently Examined and Weighed." In *The Works of James Arminius*. Translated by James Nichols, vol. 2, 706–31. London: Longman, Rees, Orme, Brown, and Green, 1828. Reprint, Grand Rapids: Baker, 1999.

Baker, Charles F. *A Dispensational Theology*. 2nd ed. Grand Rapids: Grace Bible College Publications, 1971.

Barr, James. *The Semantics of Biblical Language*. Oxford: Oxford University Press, 1961. Reprint, London: SCM, 1983.

Bauer, Walter. *A Greek-English Lexicon of the New Testament and Other Early Christian Literature*. Revised and edited by Frederick William Danker. 3rd ed. Chicago: University of Chicago Press, 2000.

Berkhof, Louis. *Systematic Theology*. 4th ed. Grand Rapids: Eerdmans, 1941. Reprint, Carlisle, PA: Banner of Truth Trust, 1958.

Blass, F., and A. Debrunner. *A Greek Grammar of the New Testament and other Early Christian Literature*. Translated and revised by Robert W. Funk. Chicago: University of Chicago Press, 1961.

Boettner, Loraine. *The Reformed Doctrine of Predestination*. 4th ed. Grand Rapids: Eerdmans, 1936.

Boice, James Montgomery. *Foundations of the Christian Faith: A Comprehensive & Readable Theology*. Revised ed. Leicester and Downers Grove, IL: Inter-Varsity, 1986.

Dana, H. E., and Julius R. Mantey. *A Manual Grammar of the Greek New Testament*. New York: Macmillan, 1927.

Dillow, Joseph C. *The Reign of the Servant Kings: A Study of Eternal Security and the Final Significance of Man*. 2nd ed. Hayesville, NC: Schoettle, 1993.

Eco, Umberto, with Richard Rorty, Jonathan Culler and Christine Brooke-Rose. *Interpretation and Overinterpretation*. Edited by Stefan Collini. New York: Cambridge University Press, 1992.

Eco, Umberto. *The Limits of Interpretation*. Indianapolis: Indiana University Press, 1990.

Grudem, Wayne. *Systematic Theology: An Introduction to Bible Doctrine*. Grand Rapids: Zondervan, 1994.

Hale, Clarence B. *The Meaning of "In Christ" in the Greek New Testament*. Dallas: SIL, 1991.

Hanko, Herman. "Total Depravity." In *The Five Points of Calvinism* by Herman Hanko, Homer Hoeksema, and Gise J. Van Baren. Grand Rapids: Reformed Free, 1980.

Hirsch, E. D,. Jr. *The Aims of Interpretation*. Chicago: University of Chicago Press, 1976.

Hirsch, E. D., Jr. *Validity in Interpretation*. New Haven, CT: Yale University Press, 1967.

Hodge, Archibald Alexander. *Popular Lectures on Theological Themes*. Philadelphia, PA: Presbyterian Board, 1887.

Hodge, Charles. *Systematic Theology*. 3 vols. London and Edinburgh: Nelson; New York: Scribner, 1871–72.

Hodges, Zane C. *Absolutely Free! A Biblical Reply to Lordship Salvation*. Dallas: Redención Viva; Grand Rapids: Academie, 1989.

Hofstadter, Douglas R. *Gödel, Escher, Bach: An Eternal Golden Braid*. New York: Basic, 1979.

Johnson, Elliott E. *Expository Hermeneutics: An Introduction*. Grand Rapids: Academie, 1990.

McDowell, Josh. *Evidence that Demands a Verdict*. N.p.: Campus Crusade, 1972.

McDowell, Josh. *More Evidence that Demands a Verdict*. N.p.: Campus Crusade, 1975.

Osbeck, Kenneth W. *Amazing Grace: 366 Inspiring Hymn Stories for Daily Devotions*. Grand Rapids: Kregel, 1990. Electronic reprint, Oak Harbor, WA: Logos, n.d.

Pink, Arthur. *The Doctrine of Salvation*. Grand Rapids: Baker, 1975.

Plantinga, Alvin. *Does God Have a Nature?* Aquinas Lecture 44. Milwaukee: Marquette University Press, 1980.

Plantinga, Alvin. *God and Other Minds: A Study of the Rational Justification of Belief in God*. London and Ithaca, NY: Cornell University Press, 1967.

Plantinga, Alvin. *God, Freedom and Evil*. New York: Harper and Row, 1974. Reprint, Grand Rapids: Eerdmans, 1978.

Robertson, A. T. *A Grammar of the Greek New Testament in the Light of Historical Research*. 4th ed. New York: Hodder and Stoughton, 1923. Reprint, Nashville, TN: Broadman, 1934.

Robinson, Haddon W. *Biblical Preaching: The Development and Delivery of Expository Messages*. Grand Rapids: Baker, 1980.

Ryrie, Charles C. *Basic Theology*. Wheaton, IL: Victor, 1986.

Schaff, Philip, ed. *The Creeds of Christendom*. 6th ed. Revised by David S. Schaff. 3 vols. New York: Harper and Row, 1931. Reprint, Grand Rapids: Baker, 1998.

Schreiner, Thomas R., and Ardel B. Caneday. *The Race Set Before Us: A Biblical Theology of Perseverance and Assurance*. Leicester and Downers Grove, IL: Inter-Varsity, 2001.

Sproul, R. C. *Chosen By God*. Wheaton, IL: Tyndale House, 1986.

Steele, David N., and Curtis C. Thomas. *The Five Points of Calvinism: Defined, Defended, Documented*. International Library of Philosophy and Theology: Biblical and Theological Studies, edited by J. Marcellus Kik. Phillipsburg, NJ: Presbyterian and Reformed, 1963.

Strong, Augustus Hopkins. *Systematic Theology: A Compendium and Commonplace-Book Designed for the Use of Theological Students*. Philadelphia, PA: Judson, 1907.

Summers, Thos. O. [Thomas Osmond]. *Systematic Theology: A Complete Body of Wesleyan Arminian Divinity*. Edited, revised and annotated by Jno. J. [John James] Tigert. Nashville, TN: Methodist Episcopal Church, South, 1888.

Turner, Nigel. *Syntax*. Vol. 3 of *A Grammar of New Testament Greek*. Edinburgh: Clark, 1963.

Wallace, Daniel B. *Greek Grammar Beyond the Basics*: An Exegetical Syntax of the New Testament. Grand Rapids: Zondervan, 1996.

Warfield, Benjamin B. "On Faith in its Psychological Aspects." In *Studies in Theology*, 313–42. New York: Oxford University Press, 1932. Reprint, Edinburgh and Carlisle, PA: Banner of Truth, 1988.

Wesley, John. "On Working out our own Salvation." In *Sermons on Several Occasions: Second Series*. N.p.: n.p., 1788. Reprinted in *The Works of John Wesley*, 3rd ed., vol. 6, 506–13. London: Wesleyan Methodist, 1872. Reprint, Grand Rapids: Baker, 1979.

Wilkin, Robert N. *Confident in Christ: Living by Faith Really Works*. Irving, TX: Grace Evangelical Society, 1999.

Winer, G. B. *A Treatise on the Grammar of the New Testament*. Translated by W. F. Moulton. Edinburgh: Clark, 1882. Reprint, Eugene, OR: Wipf and Stock, 1997.

Wines, E. C. *A Treatise on Regeneration*. Philadelphia, PA: Presbyterian Board, 1863.

Zerwick, Maximilian. *Biblical Greek Illustrated by Examples*. Translated and adapted by Joseph Smith. Rome: Pontifical Bible Institute, 1963.

PERIODICALS

Aldrich, Roy L. "The Gift of God." *Bibliotheca Sacra* 122 (July–September 1965): 248–53. Electronic reprint, Garland, TX: Galaxie, 2002.

Allen, Thomas G. "Exaltation and Solidarity with Christ: Ephesians 1.20 and 2.6." *Journal for the Study of the New Testament* 28 (October 1986): 103–20.

Anderson, David R. "The Nature of Faith." *CTS Journal* 5 (October–December 1999): 2–26.

Chafer, Lewis Sperry. "Dispensationalism." *Bibliotheca Sacra* 93 (October–December 1936): 390–449. Electronic reprint, Garland, TX: Galaxie, 2002.

Countess, Robert H. "Thank God for the Genitive." *Journal of the Evangelical Theological Society* 12 (Spring 1969): 117–22.

Denbow, Walter H. "A Note on *Ephesians* II. I." *Congregational Quarterly* 35 (January 1957): 62–64.

Nichols, Timothy R. "Reverse-Engineered Outlining: A Method for Epistolary Exegesis." *CTS Journal* 7 (April–June 2001): 16–58.

Niemelä, John H. "*If Anyone's Work Is Burned*: Scrutinizing Proof-Texts." *CTS Journal* 8 (January–March 2002): 22–42.

Sapaugh, Gregory P. "Is Faith a Gift? A Study of Ephesians 2:8." *Journal of the Grace Evangelical Society* 7 (Spring 1994): 31–43.

Townsend, Jim. "'Saved by Grace Alone—This is All my Plea' (An Exposition of Ephesians 2:8–10)." *Emmaus Journal* 7 (Winter 1998): 230–40. Electronic reprint, Garland, TX: Galaxie, 2002.

UNPUBLISHED MATERIALS

Andrew, Stephen L. "PROPER: A Free-Grace Alternative to Calvinism's TULIP and Arminianism's PEARS." Paper presented to National Teaching Pastors' Conference, Omaha, NE, October 2001.

Bumgardner, Bruce. "Obedience/Disobedience to the Gospel: Is the Will Involved in Faith?" Paper presented to National Teaching Pastors' Conference, San Juan Capistrano, CA, March 2003.

"Efficient Causality: The Traditional View of Classical Realism." http://radicalacademy.com/studentrefphil6j.htm. Accessed Feb. 20, 2004.

Marshall, Ann, and Timothy R. Nichols, "Neuter Uses of Οὗτος in Paul." Paper submitted for 305 Advanced Greek Grammar. Chafer Theological Seminary, Fall 2000.

Nichols, Timothy R. "Commands to Believe: An Objection to Passive Faith?" Paper presented to National Teaching Pastors' Conference, Omaha, NE, October 2001.

Nichols, Timothy R. "Is Faith a Decision?" Paper presented to National Teaching Pastors' Conference, San Juan Capistrano, CA, March 2002.

Smith, Dwight P. "The Act of Regeneration and its Immediate Correlates." M.A. thesis, Talbot Theological Seminary, 1979.

Vos, Geerhardus. "The Spiritual Resurrection of Believers: A Sermon on Ephesians 2:4,5." Translated by Richard B. Gaffin, Jr. http://www.kerux.com/documents/KeruxV5N1A1.asp. Accessed July 21, 2003.